SEQUOYAH

NORTH AMERICAN INDIANS OF ACHIEVEMENT

SEQUOYAH
Inventor of the Cherokee Alphabet

Jane Shumate

Senior Consulting Editor
W. David Baird
Howard A. White Professor of History
Pepperdine University

CHELSEA HOUSE PUBLISHERS
New York   Philadelphia

FRONTISPIECE The capitol building rotunda in Oklahoma City features this mural painting of Sequoyah, executed by artist Charles Bands Wilson in 1965.

ON THE COVER Sequoyah, creator of the Cherokee alphabet, devoted his life to sustaining the language and culture of a great Indian nation.

Chelsea House Publishers
EDITORIAL DIRECTOR Richard Rennert
EXECUTIVE MANAGING EDITOR Karyn Gullen Browne
EXECUTIVE EDITOR Sean Dolan
COPY CHIEF Robin James
PICTURE EDITOR Adrian G. Allen
ART DIRECTOR Robert Mitchell
MANUFACTURING DIRECTOR Gerald Levine
SYSTEMS MANAGER Lindsey Ottman
PRODUCTION COORDINATOR Marie Claire Cebrián-Ume

North American Indians of Achievement
SENIOR EDITOR Marian W. Taylor

Staff for SEQUOYAH
ASSISTANT EDITOR Margaret Dornfeld
EDITORIAL ASSISTANT Joy Sanchez
SENIOR DESIGNER Rae Grant
PICTURE RESEARCHER Lisa Kirchner
COVER ILLUSTRATOR Janet Hamlin

Printed and bound in Mexico.

First Printing

1 3 5 7 9 8 6 4 2

Library of Congress Cataloging-in-Publication Data

Shumate, Jane, 1961–
Sequoyah: inventor of the Cherokee alphabet / Jane Shumate.
p. cm. — (North American Indians of achievement)
Includes bibliographical references and index.
ISBN 0-7910-1720-6
ISBN 0-7910-1990-X (paper)
1. Sequoyah, 1770?–1843—Juvenile literature. 2. Cherokee Indians—Biography—Juvenile literature. 3. Cherokee Indians—Writing—Juvenile literature. I. Title. II. Series.
E99.C5S389 1993   93-18107
970'.00497—dc20   CIP
[B]

CONTENTS

NORTH AMERICAN INDIANS OF ACHIEVEMENT

BLACK HAWK
Sac Rebel

JOSEPH BRANT
Mohawk Chief

COCHISE
Apache Chief

CRAZY HORSE
Sioux War Chief

CHIEF GALL
Sioux War Chief

GERONIMO
Apache Warrior

HIAWATHA
Founder of the Iroquois
Confederacy

CHIEF JOSEPH
Nez Perce Leader

PETER MACDONALD
Former Chairman of the Navajo
Nation

WILMA MANKILLER
Principal Chief of the Cherokees

OSCEOLA
Seminole Rebel

QUANAH PARKER
Comanche Chief

KING PHILIP
Wampanoag Rebel

POCAHONTAS
Powhatan Peacemaker

PONTIAC
Ottawa Rebel

RED CLOUD
Sioux War Chief

WILL ROGERS
Cherokee Entertainer

SITTING BULL
Chief of the Sioux

TECUMSEH
Shawnee Rebel

JIM THORPE
Sac and Fox Athlete

SARAH WINNEMUCCA
Northern Paiute Writer and
Diplomat

Other titles in preparation

ON INDIAN LEADERSHIP

by W. David Baird

Howard A. White Professor of History
Pepperdine University

Authoritative utterance is in thy mouth, perception is in thy heart, and thy tongue is the shrine of justice," the ancient Egyptians said of their king. From him, the Egyptians expected authority, discretion, and just behavior. Homer's *Iliad* suggests that the Greeks demanded somewhat different qualities from their leaders: justice and judgment, wisdom and counsel, shrewdness and cunning, valor and action. It is not surprising that different people living at different times should seek different qualities from the individuals they looked to for guidance. By and large, a people's requirements for leadership are determined by two factors: their culture and the unique circumstances of the time and place in which they live.

Before the late 15th century, when non-Indians first journeyed to what is now North America, most Indian tribes were not ruled by a single person. Instead, there were village chiefs, clan headmen, peace chiefs, war chiefs, and a host of other types of leaders, each with his or her own specific duties. These influential people not only decided political matters but also helped shape their tribe's social, cultural, and religious life. Usually, Indian leaders held their positions because they had won the respect of their peers. Indeed, if a leader's followers at any time decided that he or she was out of step with the will of the people, they felt free to look to someone else for advice and direction.

Thus, the greatest achievers in traditional Indian communities were men and women of extraordinary talent. They were not only skilled at navigating the deadly waters of tribal politics and cultural customs but also able to, directly or indirectly, make a positive and significant difference in the daily life of their followers.

From the beginning of their interaction with Native Americans, non-Indians failed to understand these features of Indian leadership. Early European explorers and settlers merely assumed that Indians had the same relationship with their leaders as non-Indians had with their kings and queens. European monarchs generally inherited their positions and ruled large nations however they chose, often with little regard for the desires or needs of their subjects. As a result, the settlers of Jamestown saw Pocahontas as a "princess" and Pilgrims dubbed Wampanoag leader Metacom "King Philip," envisioning them in roles very different from those in which their own people placed them.

As more and more non-Indians flocked to North America, the nature of Indian leadership gradually began to change. Influential Indians no longer had to take on the often considerable burden of pleasing only their own people; they also had to develop a strategy of dealing with the non-Indian newcomers. In a rapidly changing world, new types of Indian role models with new ideas and talents continually emerged. Some were warriors; others were peacemakers. Some held political positions within their tribes; others were writers, artists, religious prophets, or athletes. Although the demands of Indian leadership altered from generation to generation, several factors that determined which Indian people became prominent in the centuries after first contact remained the same.

Certain personal characteristics distinguished these Indians of achievement. They were intelligent, imaginative, practical, daring, shrewd, uncompromising, ruthless, and logical. They were constant in friendships, unrelenting in hatreds, affectionate with their relatives, and respectful to their God or gods. Of course, no single Native American leader embodied all these qualities, nor these qualities only. But it was these characteristics that allowed them to succeed.

The special skills and talents that certain Indians possessed also brought them to positions of importance. The life of Hiawatha, the legendary founder of the powerful Iroquois Confederacy, displays the value that oratorical ability had for many Indians in power.

The biography of Cochise, the 19th-century Apache chief, illustrates that leadership often required keen diplomatic skills not only in transactions among tribespeople but also in hardheaded negotiations with non-Indians. For others, such as Mohawk Joseph Brant and Navajo Peter MacDonald, a non-Indian education proved advantageous in their dealings with other peoples.

Sudden changes in circumstance were another crucial factor in determining who became influential in Indian communities. King Philip in the 1670s and Geronimo in the 1880s both came to power when their people were searching for someone to lead them into battle against white frontiersmen who had forced upon them a long series of indignities. Seeing the rising discontent of Indians of many tribes in the 1810s, Tecumseh and his brother, the Shawnee prophet Tenskwatawa, proclaimed a message of cultural revitalization that appealed to thousands. Other Indian achievers recognized cooperation with non-Indians as the most advantageous path during their lifetime. Sarah Winnemucca in the late 19th century bridged the gap of understanding between her people and their non-Indian neighbors through the publication of her autobiography *Life Among the Piutes*. Olympian Jim Thorpe in the early 20th century championed the assimilationist policies of the U.S. government and, with his own successes, demonstrated the accomplishments Indians could make in the non-Indian world. And Wilma Mankiller, principal chief of the Cherokees, continues to fight successfully for the rights of her people through the courts and through negotiation with federal officials.

Leadership among Native Americans, just as among all other peoples, can be understood only in the context of culture and history. But the centuries that Indians have had to cope with invasions of foreigners in their homelands have brought unique hardships and obstacles to the Native American individuals who most influenced and inspired others. Despite these challenges, there has never been a lack of Indian men and women equal to these tasks. With such strong leaders, it is no wonder that Native Americans remain such a vital part of this nation's cultural landscape.

1

Taming a Wild Animal

Cherokee spokesman and scholar Sequoyah appears with his alphabet in a 1940 portrait by Robert Lindneux. Around his neck hangs a medal awarded him by the administration of President James Monroe during a trip to Washington, D.C.

One day around 1800 a young Cherokee named Sequoyah set out on a long journey. He was traveling from his home in Willstown, in what is now Alabama, to a town called Echota, in Tennessee, to see his friends and spend time with them talking, laughing, and arguing. Sequoyah was in his late twenties—by all accounts a thoughtful, inquisitive, and lively young man. He was about medium height and slender, with light, copper-colored skin, and he wore traditional Cherokee clothing: buckskin leggings, soft leather boots, a tunic that was belted at the waist and held his knife and pipe, and a bright scarf wrapped around his head. Beneath the wrap his face was handsome and confident. He had a long nose, a narrow mouth with a slight smile, and animated, piercing eyes. He walked with a limp, but his stride was quick and sure.

Sequoyah no doubt knew his path well. To his left as he walked northeast ran the Tennessee River; ahead and to the right was Lookout Mountain. A little farther beyond was a cluster of small towns where he had lived for a time as a boy. The ground he walked on, the trees he brushed, the river he heard, and the hills he saw in the distance had all belonged to his people for more than a thousand years. Cherokee territory once

covered about 40,000 square miles of land in what is now called West Virginia, Virginia, North and South Carolina, Georgia, Alabama, Tennessee, and Kentucky. This land was a mixture of mountains, rivers, hills, and valleys thickly covered with oak, maple, pine, peach, plum, and apple trees.

According to long tradition, Sequoyah was, as a Cherokee, one of the "principal people," and this was his land. Sequoyah had probably grown up learning that Kana'ti, the first man, had taught the men how to hunt bear and deer, and that Selu, the first woman, had shown the women how to grow corn and beans. His people had known how to catch the fish that swam in each stream,

This 1883 lithograph shows the rocky slope of Lookout Mountain, Tennessee. Such thickly forested, changeable landscape was typical of Cherokee country.

where to find the wild herbs that would cure illnesses, how to avoid the pools that hid the Ukte'na—treacherous, snakelike monsters with horns. Because his people knew they depended upon the land, they tried to live in harmony with it, never taking more from it than they needed. In fact, when the new corn crop was ready each year, they burned what remained from the year before because it was wrong to keep more than was necessary.

Although Sequoyah had been brought up with such traditions, much had changed since he was a boy. His people had lost almost half of their territory to the white Americans, who built houses all around, every month a little closer to the Cherokees' own homes. Cherokee women now sat indoors spinning cotton. Cherokee men now worked in fields instead of hunting. They had forgotten what Kana'ti and Selu had shown them. Many no longer even believed that they were the principal

This sketch, based on modern excavations of the Cherokee town Echota, shows two homes, summer (right) and winter, as they would have appeared during Sequoyah's childhood. A hearth in the center of the winter home kept Indian families warm.

people. As Sequoyah followed the path to Echota, he probably saw more signs of these changes: every now and then a large wooden house, a vast field of cotton, an African slave, perhaps even a missionary building.

Echota was just one of 40 or so Cherokee towns dotted throughout Cherokee country around 1800. It had once been a principal, or capital, town of the Cherokees, and Sequoyah's uncle had been an important chief there. As he approached the town, Sequoyah may have thought about what it had been like when he was a boy. The homes had been built in the traditional style: rectangular summer houses made of saplings woven together; round winter houses made of the same material and bound with a mud plaster. From them had risen the savory smell of venison or bear-meat stews and warm hominy prepared from homegrown corn. Had this been the town of his childhood, women would have been outside harvesting pumpkins, ears of corn, or squash from their garden plots, their babies in cradles swinging from branches, while the men hunted or practiced their hunting and warring skills by playing a fast-paced, violent ball game. Echota would have been filled with people.

But this could not have been what Sequoyah saw now. Echota was by this time a ruined town with only a handful of houses. If he saw any people, they were poor. They probably wore scraps of white-style cotton clothing. In rocky fields around town grew corn—not Indian corn, but rather the yellow variety favored by white Americans—and a little cotton. Outside the houses were probably chickens, maybe a cow or two.

Many years later, Sequoyah recounted the story of this day to Samuel Lorenzo Knapp, a reporter. As he told his interviewer, he eventually entered the house of his friends, where a few others joined them. Before long Sequoyah and his friends were discussing, as they so often

Guided by Indians, early settlers pass through the rivers and swamps of eastern Cherokee country. Relations between whites and Cherokees began peacefully, but grew increasingly tense as settlers failed to honor many of their agreements.

did, the white people who were bringing these changes to the Cherokees' lives.

When the Europeans had first arrived in Cherokee country more than 200 years before, Sequoyah knew that they had seemed strange to his people, but perhaps not much more so than other tribes. Anyone who was not a Cherokee was not one of the principal people and was therefore a stranger of sorts. The Cherokees lived near at least four other major tribes—Creek, Choctaw, Chickasaw, and Seminole—whom they considered very different from themselves. They dealt often with these tribes, trading or warring according to established intertribal patterns. The new white tribes had seemed like any other non-Cherokees except that they were more aggressive.

In the years following the first encounter, white traders had dealt with or even lived among the Cherokees, taking the Indians' furs in exchange for various goods, such as metal blades and whiskey. White settlers had gradually moved closer to the Cherokee heartland, and many had shown little regard for the sorts of intertribal agreements and relations that the Cherokees honored. As a result the Cherokees had often fought these settlers. The fighting had intensified and erupted into full war when Sequoyah was a boy. There had hardly been a time in his early life when his people were not fighting bloody battles.

In the past few years, though, peace had prevailed, and a new sort of white person had been mingling with the Cherokees: missionaries who wanted to teach the Indians their language and their religion. They wanted to change the Cherokees even more than the traders and settlers had, with their metal blades and whiskey and two-story houses and cotton and chickens. These missionaries wanted to teach the Cherokees how to read their "Great Book."

Unlike the Cherokees—or indeed any of the other tribes Sequoyah and his friends knew—these whites had a way of communicating silently on paper. They could put marks on a piece of paper, which, sent any distance, could somehow convey to whoever looked at it what the person making the marks had meant to say. Sequoyah's friends called these marked papers talking leaves. Sequoyah had seen one of these papers a few years earlier when a white soldier had been captured and brought to his town. The man had pulled a crumpled sheet from his pocket and had spoken from it, as though it were somehow telling him what to say.

Sequoyah's friends spoke of this miraculous skill admiringly and agreed that it was well beyond their reach. According to Sequoyah, they shook their heads and said that they would have to be content to live without this fabulous magic. The Cherokee people all spoke dialects of the same language, and they shared some words and

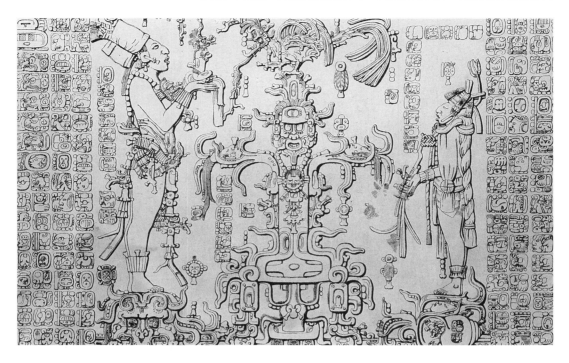

Although the Indians of North America had no written language, the Mayans, a Mexican people, had developed a complex script long before the arrival of Europeans. The Mayan panel drawn here bears a hieroglyphic inscription along its sides.

forms of sign language with other tribes, but they had no system of writing. This meant that to communicate with each other they were obliged to meet personally or send messengers. This also meant that they had no reliable way of noting their thoughts, of documenting their agreements, or of recording their history, knowledge, or legends.

In this the Cherokees were like all North American Indians of the time. But more than a thousand years before, Mayans, another group of Indians who had created a complex and highly cultured society in what is now Mexico, had developed an elaborate system of writing. When Spanish explorers reached the Mayans in the early 16th century, however, just a few years before other Spaniards reached the Cherokees, they plundered that rich, sophisticated culture. They claimed that the Mayans, who of course were not Christians, were savages. But they were nervous when they discovered that the Mayans had parchment books: for how could "savages" have books? The Spaniards were frightened and suspicious of the Mayans' "secret code." So they burned most of the Mayans' books in bonfires, saving only a few to lock away in a special archive in Rome.

When the Spanish explorer Hernando de Soto first reached the Cherokees, he saw that the homes of chiefs were covered with animal skins on which pictures had been painted to record those chiefs' conquests. Although this was not exactly writing, it was one way that the Cherokees and other North American Indians tried to preserve their history.

The woodlands Indians in the Pacific Northwest had worked out another way of preserving their history. Artists there carved portraits of their patrons' lives, similar to European coats-of-arms, into tall trunks of cedar called totem poles. One had only to look at the carvings to remember the history portrayed.

Many eastern communities, including the Cherokees and many of the Iroquois and Algonkian tribes to the north, used another device. Called *wampum*, it consisted of white and purple shells drilled, cut into beads, and strung together into strands or belts. These were woven into arrangements that acted as mnemonic devices: that is, they reminded the observer of certain events, boundaries, or agreements. They were used among different tribes for both diplomatic and trade purposes. With wampum, too, the Indians looking at the symbols already "knew" to which events they referred; they had only to remember.

The Algonkian tribes also used a form of picture writing like that of the Aztecs. It had certain symbols that did not exactly look like what they meant but that everyone agreed would mean a certain thing: for example, a spiral would mean "quickly," or a diagonal cross would mean "war." This system was much more sophisticated than wampum or totem poles.

But none of these techniques was completely reliable. To be understood, each system required that someone already know, or remember, what was first meant by a certain bead or carving or picture. But if no one remembered, Sequoyah realized, then the histories would be silent, as though nothing had ever happened. The legends—as important to the Cherokees as the Bible was to the Europeans—would be lost. And everything they knew about using the earth to nourish and cure them when they were sick would be gone. So too would be the chants of the medicine men. All his people's knowledge could be lost if not captured safely.

Sequoyah knew that the marks made by white men and women preserved ideas, information, and history securely—much as the curing process might preserve a pelt so it could be used. And he had seen that the missionaries and other whites who moved among his people had books, so he knew that whole collections of ideas could be bound together. He also knew that these whites were gradually taking over his people's land and traditional way of life. Did their "talking leaves" allow them to develop and communicate their knowledge more quickly, making them more powerful? If so, why couldn't his people do the same?

But as Sequoyah sat with his friends, he heard them voice a common Cherokee belief. They thought that this "magic" was beyond them. The Cherokees even had a legend explaining why. In the beginning, the legend went, were an Indian and a white man. The Indian, who was older, had been given a book, while the white man had been given a bow and arrow. They were both to be put to good use. But the Indian was not particularly interested in his book, and after a time the white man stole it. The Indian in turn had to take the bow and arrow and learn to survive with them. And so, the legend concluded, the Indian had forfeited his book, which now rightfully belonged to his white brother.

Sequoyah's friends shrugged and accepted this story, moving on to talk about other things. But Sequoyah brooded. As he later told Knapp, he knew that these "talking leaves" were not magic; they were simply an invention. All that inventions required was intelligence and perseverance. He himself was an artist and silversmith. He had been inventing useful, beautiful things with nothing but his hands and cleverness for years. And certainly most of the white newcomers he had seen were no more intelligent or patient than he was: many of them moved loudly through the forest; they were crude and violent and seldom even bathed. If these people could have such a marvelous thing as talking leaves, certainly the Cherokees could as well.

Sequoyah looked at his friends. Some of them were wearing white men's clothes: itchy woolen trousers, heavy boots. They were willing to wear the whites' clothes, which they did not need, but not take the truly valuable part of white culture. Sequoyah lost his temper and broke into their conversation.

"You are all fools!" he said. "Why, the thing is very easy. I can do it myself."

As his friends looked at him in surprise, Sequoyah drew a pin from his sleeve, picked up a stone, and scratched marks in its surface. "There," he said, showing them. "I can make characters which every one of you will understand."

They stared at him. Then, looking down at the marks scribbled upon the stone, marks that made no more sense than a chicken's scratchings in the dirt, they broke into laughter. They told him that he would not get far by trying to make stones talk.

Sequoyah was stung by his friends' response. But later, as he limped home, he said to himself that he knew he could make characters that would be understood. He knew that he could take his people's language and invent a way to hold it fast. It would be, he thought, like catching a wild animal and taming it.

2

Newcomers in Cherokee Country

Sequoyah was born and grew up in a period of great conflict. This conflict arose first as his people clashed with the newly arrived Europeans and intensified as the Cherokees themselves began to disagree about how to respond to the whites threatening their traditional way of life. Within Sequoyah's own family were important chiefs who differed on this matter.

Sequoyah was born about 1773 in the Cherokee town of Tuskegee—which the Indians probably pronounced more like "Taskigi," just as the name they used for themselves was closer to "Tsalagi." Tuskegee was on the Little Tennessee River, a few miles from Echota. Like Echota, its streets were evenly laid out, and its families lived along them in clusters of houses—one for winter, one for summer—with garden plots and orchards nearby.

By the time Sequoyah was a young man he was using an English name, George Gist (sometimes written "Guess" or "Guest"), as well as his Cherokee name, because his father was white. No one is sure who Sequoyah's father was. Some historians believe that he was Nathaniel Gist, a Virginia diplomat and soldier who had been among the Cherokees since the 1750s. In

A Native American woman travels with her infant. When Sequoyah was a small child, his mother probably carried him in a cradleboard similar to the one pictured here.

An artist's reconstruction shows a Cherokee town as it might have looked around the time of Sequoyah's birth. Town meetings, attended by women and men, took place in the large council house at left.

Virginia he owned a plantation and was a friend of George Washington's—he was even said to have once rescued the president from drowning. Others, however, believe that Sequoyah's father was a man named George Gist, a Dutch peddler who traded with the Cherokees. Gist may have wanted to join with Sequoyah's mother, Wurteh, to form a close bond with the Indians so that they would trust him and help him with his business. Whoever Sequoyah's father was, he left the small family when Sequoyah was an infant, and the boy grew up with his mother.

Many white men married or joined with Indian women in order to establish a strong link to their tribes. This was especially true of the Cherokees, among whom women played important roles and were well respected. They shared the tribe's labor with the men and took part in tribal decisions.

While the men defended the tribe, hunted, and fished, the women worked in the village, tending the crops and transforming all the tribe's raw goods—the fruits, grains, and vegetables they pulled from the earth and the game the men brought home—into the products the tribe depended upon. Like the other women in Tuskegee, Wurteh would have roasted, boiled, or barbecued meat: deer, bear, pork, fish, turkey, and other fowl. In addition to corn, which she would have boiled or roasted and turned into cakes, mush, or bread, she and the other women grew beans, peas, squash, potatoes, and pumpkins. Their foods were served on flat baskets made of split canes or in earthenware pottery. The women made these items as well as clothing and household furnishings: woven baskets, seats, and brightly colored rugs decorated with pictures of animals, birds, and flowers.

To perform these tasks while caring for their small children, Wurteh and the other women developed a simple system. The babies spent most of their first year or two in cradleboards—wooden boards with tight-fitting pouches of animal hide—where they were safe and warm. Their mothers took these cradleboards wherever they went, often hanging them in the branches of trees near the fields where they worked. Here Sequoyah and the other babies would swing gently, sleeping or watching the women in the fields or the birds, animals, and branches rustling around them.

Because the women were responsible for so much of the tribe's well-being, they had a voice in its government. A council of women discussed matters of importance to the tribe and conveyed their opinions to the men's council, strongly influencing tribal decisions. Women sometimes took part in war, and those who particularly distinguished themselves for their wisdom or bravery were called War Women or Beloved Women.

Furthermore, family relations and social status were determined not by the father or by both mother and father, as in our culture today, but by the mother alone. She was the head of the household. A couple were married in a simple and brief ceremony in which the woman presented the man with an ear of corn and he presented her with an animal he had hunted, representing their respective contributions to the family's livelihood. The man either built a house for them, which was then considered the woman's house, or he himself moved to her home and lived there with her family. The children of the couple were considered not part of their father's family but part of their mother's. Their mother's brothers, in fact, were more important in the children's upbringing than their father.

Through his mother, Sequoyah belonged to an important Cherokee family, the Paint clan, one of the seven Cherokee clans. His mother's brothers were distinguished chiefs and some of the most important figures among the Cherokees in the late 18th century: Doublehead, Old

The mothers of the seven clans stand before a sacred fire in this painting by Cherokee artist Dorothy Sullivan. Sequoyah belonged to the Paint clan, represented by the woman third from the right.

British colonists, assisted by a surveyor, measure off land for settlement. The European attitude toward property differed vastly from that of the Indians, who regarded the land as a great provider that flourished best when left unfenced and uncultivated.

Tassel, Pumpkin Boy, Tahlonteskee, and John Jolly. These chiefs, deliberating for hours with the chiefs of other villages, would make the tribe's overall decisions. They were to exert great influence on the way Sequoyah viewed the world—most significantly how he viewed the world of the Cherokees as it faced the world of the white newcomers.

By the time Sequoyah was born, the Cherokees had been intricately involved with Europeans for more than a hundred years. The Spanish explorer de Soto, following the 1492 voyage of Italian navigator Christopher Columbus, had marched through Cherokee country in 1540. In his wake, de Soto left a path of plundered and burned villages, murdered Indians, and—most devastating of all—deadly European diseases to which the Indians had no natural immunity and no cure. After the Spaniards, the Cherokees saw few Europeans for more than a century. Then one day in 1673, English settlers from

Virginia arrived in Echota and asked to trade goods with them.

This trade would have a great influence on the traditional Cherokee way of life. English, and later French and Spanish, traders mostly wanted the bear and deer skins the Indians were so skilled at getting. For these skins the Europeans exchanged metal hoes and hatchets, iron skillets, firearms, clothing, and whiskey, which gradually replaced the Indians' traditional goods. Another consequence of this trade was settlement. As trading routes opened, settlers arrived, building houses and farms on territory traditionally reserved by the Indians for hunting.

The Europeans—like anyone else of that era—understood only the world they already knew. In that world, civilized people were Christian, wore certain clothing, followed certain customs of acquiring property or marrying, were ruled by kings and other clearly organized forms of government (mostly made up of men), and lived in cities or on highly cultivated farms.

The Indians had different ideas. They held religious beliefs that often concerned the land and not a single god, they believed women should be involved in government, they allowed political decisions to develop out of lengthy group discussion rather than a single ruler's opinion, and they did not believe in fully exploiting the land around them. The Cherokees, for example, thought that vast tracts of land should be reserved for hunting. They believed that the animals on that land belonged to them, just as they believed that the whites owned the cattle and chickens they kept in small pens.

The Indians' way of living was incomprehensible to the Europeans. Because the Indians did not fit their idea of civilized people, the Europeans decreed them savage and did not believe that they had any justifiable claim

Seven Cherokee chiefs prepare for their long journey to England, where they would demonstrate their allegiance to King George II.

to the land. Until it was properly cultivated, settled upon, and exploited in European fashion, it was not, in their eyes, really owned. The representatives of England, France, and Spain therefore settled upon the land as they liked, despite the Indians, and often claimed it as their own.

But the Europeans themselves did not always agree on who had the right to claim land in this manner. In this they found the Indians helpful, for the various tribes often argued over territory or other issues, raiding each other's towns and taking scalps. Different tribes became allied with different groups of European traders and settlers and, supplied with foreign arms and ammunition, fought each other.

The Cherokees, who had first been approached by British traders in 1673, were allied with Great Britain for most of the following century. In 1730 a delegation of Cherokee chiefs traveled to England, where they pledged allegiance to King George II, kneeling before him and laying at his feet "the Crown of the Cherokee Nation," with four enemy scalps and five eagle tails. They swore to trade only with England and to assist the king in his battles against the French. To seal their agreement with the king, Chief Oukanaekah left behind an array of eagle feathers, saying, "This is our way of talking, which is the same thing to us as your letters in the book are to you, and to your beloved men we deliver these feathers in confirmation of all we have said."

The Cherokees consequently became involved in a war between Britain and France in 1754, largely over trade routes around present-day Ohio. This conflict, known as the French and Indian War, ended in 1763 with the defeat of the French and left Britain in control of most of the eastern Indian lands. The English government, fearing further tensions between Indians and settlers, who continued to encroach upon Indian territory, promptly passed the Proclamation of 1763, prohibiting English citizens from moving onto any more of the Indians' lands. But the settlers ignored their government's prohibition and continued to move into Cherokee territory. By 1768 so many settlers had moved beyond the prescribed border that another one had to be drawn, decreasing Cherokee hunting grounds. And in 1770 yet another border was drawn up in a treaty—this one cutting the Cherokees off from most of their land in Virginia and West Virginia. This happened several more times, and in 1775 several old chiefs made a particularly disastrous sale to the Americans, the Henderson Purchase, yielding much of their land in Tennessee and all of it in Kentucky.

The Cherokees resisted each one of these "treaties" but were compelled to agree, mostly because they saw that settlers would arrive whether they were permitted or not. Each time the Cherokees agreed to a treaty, they were promised by the settlers that this would be the last. In these treaties, the British government seemed to have little control over its subjects, the frontier families, who felt entitled to this "unused" Indian land.

The Cherokees grew increasingly angry as they watched the land they had held for thousands of years gradually slip into the newcomers' hands. The calamitous Henderson Purchase so angered some young Cherokee chiefs—among them several of Sequoyah's uncles—that tension began to develop among the Cherokees themselves. Meanwhile, anger was developing between the English settlers and their government across the sea. Sequoyah was born just as these conflicts reached a peak.

3

▿▿▿

"We Have No Place To Hunt On"

By the time the revolutionary war broke out between the rebellious settlers and the British government in 1776, there was a large movement among various Indian tribes to join together from Canada to the Gulf of Mexico and push the white settlers out. They believed that if they attacked the settlers from the west while the British attacked them from the east, the settlers would doubtless be defeated and leave. Although many Cherokee chiefs wished to stay out of the war, the small group angered by the 1775 sale of land was eager to fight, so in June, with British arms and support, they began to raid the settlers along their borders. A chief named Dragging Canoe was the leader of this group, and among his eager followers were Sequoyah's uncles Doublehead and Pumpkin Boy.

In July 1776, when Sequoyah was about three years old, several hundred of these chiefs' warriors advanced upon a white American settlement near the Great Island of the Holston, about 100 miles upriver from Tuskegee. The settlers, however, had been warned by the Cherokees' Beloved Woman Nancy Ward, who, with many others, wished to avoid bloodshed. After a brief battle, the Indians

An Indian ball player brandishes his equipment: two sticks made of wood, each with one end bent into a loop and strung with a shallow pocket of animal skin. The sticks were used to hurl a ball between goalposts set up at either end of a long playing field.

33

were repulsed, but the next day another group attacked the settlement of Chatauga, about 50 miles southeast of Tuskegee. There, too, they were defeated, but they captured a woman and little boy and carried them back to Tuskegee.

According to Cherokee blood law, a loss of life must be repaid with that of the killer or one of his people. The Cherokees had suffered terrible losses in these battles with the Americans. Thus, according to tradition, they were entitled to torture and burn at the stake their war captives unless the Beloved Women (also called War Women) chose to spare the captives, sometimes adopting them into their families. In Tuskegee the Cherokees voted to burn the little boy at the stake and were about to execute the woman as well. At the last minute, however, Nancy Ward again intervened and rescued her.

In the meantime, a coalition of American frontier colonies bordering Cherokee territory—Virginia, North Carolina, South Carolina, and Georgia—organized to attack the Cherokees. Throughout the late summer they moved in on the Cherokee heartland from different directions, leaving behind them a path of smoking villages, burned or slashed crops, and dead bodies. Before the Americans reached Sequoyah's village in the fall, however, the Cherokees sued for peace.

But one morning the people of Tuskegee awoke to the smell of smoke and the sound of gunfire and screams. Colonial soldiers, disregarding the truce, were retaliating for the execution of the boy from Chatauga and were storming the village, torching the houses, slashing the crops, and killing women, men, and children. Soon the town had been burned to the ground. Sequoyah, his mother, his uncles, and the other frightened villagers could only wait until the Americans had left, then creep back to salvage what they could.

In the spring of 1777 the Cherokees reached a new peace with the colonists, but in exchange they lost about 5 million acres—most of their holdings in South Carolina, along with large parts of North Carolina and Tennessee. Sequoyah's uncle, Chief Old Tassel, a mild but determined man, although angered by the Americans, favored peace. He probably expressed the view of most Indians when he said, according to an account by an observer from a neighboring tribe, "You say: Why do not the Indians till the ground and live as we do? May we not, with equal propriety, ask: Why do not the white people hunt and live as we do? . . . We wish, however, to be at peace with you, and to do as we would be done by."

But this new loss so angered Dragging Canoe and his supporters that they swore they would not have this "peace." Cherokee tribal decisions, however, were absolute. If, after lengthy discussion, the vast majority agreed, then the tribe's decision was official. Those who still disagreed were entitled to their opinion, but they were obliged to withdraw from the tribe. Dragging Canoe and his followers—among them Sequoyah's uncles Doublehead and Tahlonteskee—moved to the Chickamauga Creek. It is uncertain where Sequoyah and his mother lived, but Echota and Chickamauga were close to each other, so he probably grew up having contact with both.

Even after the 1777 treaty, however, the American settlers continued to trespass on Cherokee lands. Old Tassel, for his part, attempted to solve the problem diplomatically, sending the following message to a government official: "Your people . . . are daily pushing us out of our lands. We have no place to hunt on. Your people have built houses within one day's walk of our towns. We don't want to quarrel. . . . We are the first people that ever lived on this land; it is ours."

Realizing that Old Tassel's peaceful efforts were futile, the Chickamaugans responded with violence, attacking settlements and taking scalps and captives. In return for such raids, the settlers destroyed the Chickamaugans' own towns in 1779. The Indians established a new settlement downriver, which they called the Five Lower Towns; from here the rebels continued to wage bloody raids against the settlers. Old Tassel, increasingly irritated with the rebels, continued to try to solve disputes peacefully.

Thus, Sequoyah spent the first years of his life amid bloodshed and conflict not only between his people and the whites but among members of his own family. As a small boy he doubtless overheard his uncles Doublehead and Old Tassel arguing about the Americans and how the Cherokees should respond to them. But although they argued, they shared an attachment to their tribe's traditions and beliefs; along with Wurteh, they carefully taught Sequoyah the customs of the Cherokees.

Like other small Cherokee children, Sequoyah would have played in the fields and woods and streams around him, and he would have been told the ancient Cherokee legends. He knew that the rocks and trees and waters were filled with spirits—the Nunnéhi who lived forever; the Yunwi Tsunsdí, or Little People, whose beautiful hair grew to their toes and who helped lost children find their way home; or mischievous Détsata, who had run away as a little boy and now lived with a band of other children, throwing pebbles at hunters and sometimes stealing their arrows.

Sequoyah would have been told about Kana'ti and Selu, the first man and woman. He learned that the earth was like a huge dish floating on a sea of water and hanging from the sky by four cords, which would snap when the earth became worn out, dropping it into the sea. Sequoyah also learned how diseases came to be: in the old days, the

A 17th-century Dutch engraving shows Indians surrounding a herd of deer. The Indians of the Southeast did not work on horseback, as pictured here, but on foot.

animals became so furious with humans for hunting and killing them that each of them gave the humans one disease. The deer, for example, decided that if a hunter did not beg pardon from the soul of a deer he had killed, he would become crippled. But the plants and trees, hearing about the diseases the animals had caused and feeling sorry for humans, agreed to give humans the cures. These the shaman, or medicine man, knew. This was one of the ways in which the Cherokees, the land, and the animals lived together in harmony.

When Sequoyah was a little older, he helped Wurteh in the garden and cornfields, hoeing, tending, and harvesting the long rows of vegetables. His mother kept some horses and cows in the woods nearby, and Sequoyah soon learned how to take care of them, taming the colts and breaking them in for riding.

He was an inventive boy and often amused himself or made his tasks easier by creating things. As a small child he made little houses of sticks in the forest, but when he was older, he constructed various milking devices for his mother and a small wooden house over a stream to keep the cows' milk cold. He also carved animals out of wood and drew pictures of animals and people, mixing colors

Indian women wave and bang pots to frighten away birds trying to feed on their corn. To protect their crops, the Cherokees also built night bonfires and houses for purple martins, which attack blackbirds and crows.

out of crushed bark, berries, and leaves.

Throughout Sequoyah's childhood, however, violence between Chickamaugans and settlers constantly shattered the peace. The boy would hear reports of Cherokee neighbors who had been killed by the settlers, or he would see the fresh scalps of whites triumphantly brandished by returning raiders. Finally, when Sequoyah was about 12, his uncle Old Tassel and a delegation of Cherokee chiefs met with representatives of the new United States at Hopewell, about 100 miles southeast of Echota. There American officials said that the revolutionary war had finally ended with Great Britain's defeat and that the United States now wanted peace with the Indians, too.

Old Tassel, the beloved chief of Echota, told the Americans that if no more Indian lands were taken, the Cherokees and the whites could live peaceably side by side. The Americans promised that they would take no more land, and so both sides were contented. Most of the Indians hoped that the Treaty of Hopewell would at last put an end to the bloodshed and the steady encroachment on their land.

But the new U.S. government had no more control over its settlers than had the British government before it. Whites continued to move onto Cherokee land, now very close to Echota and the Lower Towns. In 1788 the U.S. Congress had to issue a proclamation prohibiting further intrusions and warning settlers that they were risking their lives.

And so they were. For the Chickamaugans ignored the Treaty of Hopewell just as the American settlers did, responding to each fresh intrusion on their territory with a violent raid. Throughout these raids and counterraids, Old Tassel did his best to keep peace and deal diplomatically. But in 1788 disaster struck: rebellious settlers who had formed their own "state," called Franklin, invaded

Echota. Everyone fled except Old Tassel, his co-chief Hanging Maw, and several other men. The Indians waved a flag of truce, but the invaders murdered them all. This outrage struck the Cherokee people deeply and eventually became a legend. Sequoyah remembered hearing that when the frightened people returned after the invasion, they found Hanging Maw's body eaten by vultures but that Old Tassel's body remained as it had been, his hand still gripping the flag and a peaceful smile upon his face.

The murders shocked even the Chickamaugans. Doublehead, Tahlonteskee, and Pumpkin Boy vowed revenge, and the raiding took on fresh energy. With their beloved leader gone, many Cherokees of Echota moved closer to the Chickamaugans' Lower Towns and renewed their relations with the rebels.

Sequoyah, then 15, was still too young to fight; he had just begun his training. Like other Cherokee boys (and sometimes girls), he learned to be patient, to endure hunger, and to bear and witness pain stoically. He was shown how to use the spear, tomahawk, and bow and arrow. He was made to sit for days near a river or in the woods so that he could observe the habits of animals, listen to their sounds, and learn to be noiseless. When he grew old enough to join the men on a hunt, he would have to go through their rituals: cleansing himself morning and evening in the river, praying, and apologizing to the souls of the deer he had killed.

Helping to train a warrior and keeping him in shape was the Cherokees' ball game, a fast-paced and demanding sport resembling lacrosse but much more violent. Before the ball game, players endured a long period of ritual cleansing, abstinence, and dancing. The period also included a painful rite in which the players' bodies were scratched with thorns or quills into almost 300 bleeding lines, after which the boys and men leaped into the river

Indians all over the Southeast played this spirited ball game, a model for modern-day lacrosse. Beyond providing entertainment, the game had a symbolic function and required two or three days of ritual preparation. Here, one team's members have painted their bodies white.

to purify themselves. In the ball game, as in warfare and hunting, young Cherokee men distinguished themselves by their speed, endurance, skill, and strength.

Sequoyah learned to be an excellent hunter, providing his mother with pelts to use or sell. But at some point in his early life he suffered a terrible blow. Either through a hunting accident or through illness, he became crippled in one leg. He may even have believed that the fault was his—that, after a successful hunt, he had forgotten to ask a deer's pardon. Most likely, though, Sequoyah's affliction was the result of polio. Like smallpox and gonorrhea, this was a disease brought by the Europeans, for which the

Indians had no cure.

When Sequoyah became sick, the shaman—who served as doctor, priest, keeper of tradition, and spiritual authority—would have come to his house to dispel any witches or wild creatures determined to cause trouble and death. The shaman probably concocted an herbal remedy for Sequoyah, and he may have had Sequoyah sit for hours in a hothouse to sweat the evil out, or lie naked on a bearskin outside, and then plunge into an icy river. But despite all this, Sequoyah—and many other Indians with diseases beyond the shamans' scope—remained ill, recovering finally with one leg permanently shriveled.

By the time Sequoyah was about 18, the U.S. government had grown stronger. Determined to control the nation's settlers and reach a fair peace with its Indians, President George Washington invited the Cherokees to a treaty meeting at White's Fort on the Holston River in July 1791.

In this meeting the United States established official boundaries to Cherokee land, proclaimed "perpetual peace," forbade the unlawful entry of settlers onto Cherokee territories, and promised that anyone who broke Cherokee or U.S. laws would be tried by those governments, respectively. This treaty became the foundation of Washington's policy toward Native Americans. He believed that justice should be dispensed impartially, commerce with the Indians should be promoted, any purchases of their lands should be orderly, and—perhaps most important for the Cherokees—that they should be "led to a greater degree of civilization." By this Washington meant that the Cherokees should learn to herd, rather than hunt, animals; to farm on smaller, more efficient plots of land; and, ultimately, to seem more like the white settlers around them.

After more than a decade of warfare, most Cherokees

Revolutionary war general George Washington (second from left) monitors the Battle of Yorktown in 1781. As the first U.S. president, Washington hoped to maintain peaceful relations with the Indians by setting up boundaries "beyond which we will endeavor to restrain our People from Hunting and Settling."

were ready to accept these terms. But Dragging Canoe and the other Chickamaugans had no interest in becoming more like the whites; moreover, they still did not believe that those whites had any right to be there. Although the Chickamaugans attended the 1791 meeting at White's Fort, they scorned the treaty's terms. The raiding continued.

In 1792, however, Dragging Canoe died, and Old Tassel's nephew, John Watts, became the new Chickamaugan leader. Watts moved his people's headquarters south to Willstown, where Sequoyah also moved. Without Dragging Canoe, the Chickamaugans lost some of their impetus, but they still were angry and violent, continuing to attack settlers who ignored official boundaries. Sequoyah's uncles Doublehead and Pumpkin Boy were, in fact, responsible for one of the most shocking acts to occur on the frontier: having attacked and scalped two white men in Kentucky, they cut flesh from their bones, roasted it, and ate it. They must have seemed to their own people more frightening than any American intruder.

The U.S. government finally decided it had to protect its frontier people and establish peace. In 1794, American troops stormed the Chickamaugans' towns. After resisting white encroachments for nearly 20 years, the rebels at last were defeated. By then everyone seemed to have had enough of bloodshed. As Bloody Fellow, one of the chiefs present at the subsequent treaty meeting, said, "I want peace, that we may . . . sleep in our houses, and rise in peace on both sides."

By this time Sequoyah was about 20. In the years since his birth, the Cherokees, once united against the white settlers, had become divided into two factions. Sequoyah grew up between them. His uncle Old Tassel believed that the American settlers were wrong, but he preferred to try to live with them rather than embroil his people in a losing battle. Sequoyah's uncles Doublehead, Pumpkin Boy, and Tahlonteskee, on the other hand, were willing to die for control of their land.

At the end of the 18th century, the Cherokees' bloody conflict with the Americans seemed to have finally ended. But the division among themselves would only widen. Sequoyah had grown up in the midst of one conflict and was to spend his early manhood in the midst of the other.

4

▽ ▽ ▽

A "Civilized" Tribe?

During this new period of peace, Sequoyah lived in Willstown, in what is now Alabama. Like Echota before it, Willstown had become a center of Cherokee government, for the Chickamaugan chiefs were strong leaders, and despite their defeat, they had earned the tribe's respect. Sequoyah spent his twenties and early thirties among these Lower Town people in an atmosphere of confusion and change.

Although the fighting between Cherokees and white Americans had ceased by 1794, a new, more subtle threat was emerging. This threat was contained in Washington's 1791 policy—considered humane by most Americans— that the Indians should be "led to a greater degree of civilization." The new U.S. government believed that the Indians did have some claim to their lands and that Indians and white Americans could live side by side—but only if the Indians adopted the ways of the whites around them. To the Indians this meant giving up warfare, replacing hunting with farming, and moving from their small, close-knit villages to scattered frontier farms.

In 1796, Washington appointed an agent, Benjamin Hawkins, to provide the southern Indians with farming equipment and domestic goods. Hawkins soon reported many signs of "civilization": Cherokees were planting

Two Cherokees bear tools symbolic of their experience—a peace pipe and a gun—in this drawing by George Catlin, who spent many years documenting Native Americans and their culture. These chiefs posed for him at their new home in Arkansas Territory.

Benjamin Hawkins, federal agent to the Creeks from 1796 to 1816, was a firm believer in Indian rights. He also supported the assimilationist policies put forth by the early U.S. government.

corn, cotton, and orchards; raising fowl, hogs, and cattle; spinning cotton into thread. He concluded that the Indians were beginning to make "progress."

U.S. agents brought more than spinning wheels, cotton seeds, and hoes to Cherokee country. To teach the Indians trades, the agents also brought craftsmen: blacksmiths, carpenters, weavers, and wheelwrights. From a white metalsmith Sequoyah learned the basics of smithwork, but he soon surpassed his instructor's skills. Using the silver that filled the hills around him, he began to make rings, ornamented headbands, breastplates, necklaces, and ankle bells, as well as bridles and other functional objects. He developed a thriving business.

While building his silver trade, Sequoyah began to see

the need for another skill. As a smith he accepted commissions for work. He needed a way to remember not only what work was wanted but also who wanted it and how much it would cost. Some of this he could easily solve: he drew well and often made a sketch of what was to be done. He even quickly sketched the person wanting it. But to record the cost Sequoyah had to invent his own system. If the price, for example, was four dollars, Sequoyah drew a line and then four circles. But this was awkward and imprecise.

He also needed a way to mark his work—of which he was justifiably proud—to show potential clients who had made it. So he went to his friend Charles Hicks, who, like Sequoyah, was part white but who also read and wrote in English and worked as an interpreter for Return

Return Meigs served as agent to the Cherokee nation from 1801 until his death in 1823. Meigs showed sympathy for the Indians but felt that their best hope lay in the adoption of white ways.

Christian efforts to convert the Native American population began early and accompanied the whites' expansion westward. Here, three Roman Catholic missionaries direct the construction of a mission in Indian Territory.

Meigs, the new government agent. Hicks showed Sequoyah how to mark his name, both "Sequoyah" and "George Gist," and Sequoyah, carefully copying Hicks's marks, was thereafter able to etch his name on his work.

But Hicks may well have pointed out that by this time Sequoyah could simply learn English himself. For in 1799, Little Turkey, the chief who had replaced Old Tassel, had proposed in a council meeting that the Cherokees accept another form of cultural change: white schooling. Most of the chiefs at the council agreed, believing that much of the whites' knowledge and power came from their "Great Book." So in 1801 missionaries from the Moravian church set up a school in Springplace, about 40 miles from the Lower Towns, to teach reading, writing, and arithmetic.

Chief Doublehead and his brother Tahlonteskee, however, refused to have any such school in the Lower Towns. Although they accepted the hoes, looms, and other goods provided by the U.S. government, they mistrusted this more subtle "gift." They knew that these missionaries would not teach the Cherokees only about their letters and numbers; they would also teach about their god.

Accounts suggest that Sequoyah shared his uncles' suspicion of the missionaries and their language, and certainly he had no love for the whites, who had destroyed his town and killed so many of his people. It was at about this time that Sequoyah traveled to Echota and began to see even more clearly how altered his homeland was, with its cleared lands, raw earth, strange new houses, and penned-in animals. His people, he may have thought, had made enough concessions. Like his uncles, he had no interest in the whites' language or their god.

By the early 1800s, Sequoyah's uncle Doublehead had become the most important Cherokee chief. Prominent in earlier warfare with the United States, he had earned the regard of his people and the grudging respect of American government officials. In an 1805 letter to his superior, U.S. agent Return Meigs said of Doublehead:

> This man . . . is exerting himself to live in a stile of some degree of taste; at the same time he is a vindictive, bloody minded Savage . . . [who would] set his foot on the neck of anything that may oppose itself to his ill founded pride. He is a man of small stature, compact and well formed, very dark skin, small piercing black eyes, the fixture of which when engaged in conversation are as immovable as diamonds set in metal.

Meigs and the other U.S. agents, whose job it was to supply the Cherokees with goods and to encourage their "progress," decided that Doublehead was the man to deal with. The Cherokees traditionally made tribal decisions through long discussions, sometimes among hundreds of chiefs and other members of the tribe. Unlike the white Americans, the Cherokees had no single leader who could represent their interests. But the U.S. agents found it easier to talk to just one or two top chiefs rather than to hundreds—especially when these top chiefs might help the United States get what it wanted.

For a decade after the Chickamaugan defeat, the agents had promoted the Cherokees' "civilization." But in the early 1800s this policy quietly began to change. In 1803, President Jefferson acquired for his rapidly growing nation a vast parcel of western land called the Louisiana Purchase. The following year, he sent a group of explorers, led by Meriwether Lewis and William Clark, on an expedition to the West. They returned with reports of a wild, rich land that the United States might also claim—although it was occupied by other Indian tribes. With all these resources in the West, Jefferson began to think that the eastern Indians might not need to become "civilized," after all. Perhaps they would be better off moving west.

Thus, many of the meetings between Jefferson's agents and Doublehead involved not how the Cherokees could become even more "civilized" but how they could exchange their eastern homelands for untapped land— filled with game they could hunt—in the West. The Cherokees found this idea paradoxical. As a missionary once described it,

> The Indians say they don't know how to understand their Father the President. A few years ago he sent them a plough and a hoe—said it was not good for his red children to hunt—they must cultivate the earth. Now he tells them there is good hunting at the Arkansas; if they will go there he will give them rifles.

Doublehead could see that no matter how much his people changed—farming, spinning cotton, learning English—it was not their "civilization" that the whites wanted but their land. The whites had defeated him once before, and they were growing stronger as more Europeans poured over and pushed westward across the American continent. They would eventually get what they wanted. In the meantime, Doublehead intended to get what he could in exchange.

Unfortunately, most of what Doublehead got he kept for himself. He yielded land in North Carolina and Tennessee; in 1804 he traded away much of Georgia; in 1805 he sold even more of Tennessee. With each "sale" Doublehead—acting secretly with only a few other chiefs—profited, gaining money, guns, goods and equipment, and "permanent" titles to choice pieces of land.

By 1807 other members of the tribe realized that Doublehead was betraying them. Especially angry were the younger chiefs, who knew they were being cheated out of their birthright by an older man who had little to lose. Many of these younger chiefs—Sequoyah's generation and younger—were either married to white women or were the children of Cherokee women and white men. They had learned English and white customs and had acquired private property, some of it inherited from their white fathers. This, for a people who believed in communal property and who were traditionally attached not to their fathers but to their mothers, was new. Some of these younger chiefs were even becoming rich, owning large farms and black slaves. As full participants in the "civilization" program, they would have a lot to lose if the Cherokees' land were sold, and they were outraged by Doublehead's deals.

And they had other reasons for considering Doublehead an unfit chief. Not only was he deceitful, but in the war with the Americans he had eaten human flesh. More recently he had beaten his pregnant wife to death. How, the younger Cherokees may have thought, could their "civilization" proceed with a leader like this?

They decided that Doublehead must die. In this decision they had the support of Cherokee law, which said that anyone who takes a life must pay for it with his own life (or that of a family member). It also said that anyone who yielded Cherokee land without the tribe's consent could be killed without retaliation.

One of the men selected to assassinate Doublehead was a young chief named The Ridge. The group went to a tavern where the old chief was expected. When he arrived after dark, The Ridge approached, blew out the candle, shot him in the head, and fled.

But the bullet went in under Doublehead's ear and out through his jaw. He survived and hid in a nearby house. The Ridge and an accomplice found him and shot him again. They wrestled him, they beat him, but still he did not go down. Finally, The Ridge seized his hatchet and split open the old chief's head. Two of Sequoyah's uncles had now been murdered: one, who had favored peace with the Americans, was killed by them; the other, who had long fought the Americans, was killed by his own people.

With Doublehead dead, Meigs had to turn to the old chief's allies—Black Fox, Tahlonteskee, and John Jolly—to persuade them to sell their land and move west. Like Doublehead, they accepted bribes, and in 1809 they proposed to the Cherokee Council that the tribe leave.

By this time, however, the young chiefs had begun organizing themselves against such ideas. By his own account, dictated to Superintendent of Indian Affairs Thomas McKenney some time after the dispute, The Ridge responded to the old chiefs' proposal:

African slaves go about their daily tasks on an Arkansas plantation. In the early 1800s more than 1,000 Cherokees sought refuge in Arkansas Territory.

I scorn this movement of a few men to unsettle the nation
and trifle with our attachment to the land of our fore-
fathers! Look abroad over the face of this country—along
the rivers, the creeks, and their branches, and you will
behold the dwellings of the people who repose in content
and security. Why is this grand scheme projected to
lead away to another country the people who are happy
here?

The younger chiefs won the day and swiftly deposed
those who had suggested removal. By early 1810, several
of the older chiefs, including Tahlonteskee, knowing that
they were unwelcome (and perhaps fearing assassination),
left for new land in the west. More than a thousand
people went with them to start the western Cherokee
Nation. One group, later known as the Old Settlers,
followed Tahlonteskee to what is now Arkansas; another
group followed a Cherokee leader named Chief Bowl to
Texas.

The proposal to move west helped the younger chiefs
gather support. With the old chiefs removed, the others
were able to unite those Cherokees who were still
floundering under the "civilization" program and
wondering what it meant to be a Cherokee when the old
way of life was forbidden. Meeting at Willstown—once
the center of the Chickamaugan resistance movement—
the newly unified chiefs agreed that being a true
Cherokee meant being committed to staying on tribal
land. Therefore, they proclaimed, those who proposed to
sell the land were not true Cherokees (although most of
the old chiefs, in contrast to the young chiefs, were
full-bloods). This new generation believed that in order
to keep their lands they must convince the U.S. government that they were prepared to live alongside white
Americans. To do this they were willing to adopt even
more white ways, including English, Christianity,
capitalism, agriculture, and a limited democracy.

Sequoyah probably did not agree with these decisions. He thought that being Cherokee meant more than occupying land; it meant believing in the Cherokee traditions, in the principal people, in the ancient magic of the shamans, in the stories that had been told for centuries. The real threat to the Cherokee people was not the disappearance of their ancestral lands but the disappearance of their ancestral beliefs. Although Sequoyah loved the land, he felt that the Cherokees' spirit lived in their minds and their words. It was the Cherokee language that held the stories and magic incantations and beliefs and history of his people. Language, he could see, was like a box that contained these things. And each day that another Cherokee child learned to speak and write English and to worship a foreign god, a little more of the Cherokee tradition slipped out of the box.

Sequoyah had no interest in the white man's beliefs, language, and writing. He hoped to preserve Cherokee culture by inventing a writing that his people could have as their own. He would make a written language to capture the Cherokee world before it slipped away forever.

5

Shake the War Clubs

When Sequoyah began to think about inventing a system of writing, he was in his mid-thirties. His mother had died by then, and most of his uncles had either died or moved away. Only John Jolly still lived nearby, on an island in the Tennessee River. Sequoyah had not yet married, although he was admired for his skills and considered very handsome, despite his lameness. Perhaps, having missed out on warfare—through which young Cherokee men distinguished themselves—he was not yet ready to settle down.

Sequoyah instead spent time developing his business and socializing. He became a famous storyteller, and friends drank with him for hours as he smoked his pipe and told ancient Cherokee legends. He often drew or painted, creating wonderful likenesses of cows, horses, deer, houses, and people.

In his spare time Sequoyah began trying to capture language, thinking he could do it in the same way he caught people's faces or animals' forms on bark. He started by drawing quick pictures to represent words, making a simple diagram for "house," for example, or "tree." He did his drawings on birchbark with charcoal sticks. Soon he had accumulated piles of these little

A Cherokee hunter sets out on an expedition. The War of 1812 inspired thousands of Cherokees to move west in search of peace.

picture-words. But his work was interrupted by two movements that swept through the Cherokee Nation.

Although many Cherokees had embraced the whites' ways, numerous others wished to but could not. There were not enough plows, spinning wheels, mills, cows, or English teachers to go around, and those who missed out found it difficult to change on their own. By 1809 the Cherokees had divided into two types of families: about 300 had adopted white ways and were prospering, and about 2,000 were barely getting by.

Families often went hungry when crops failed, and many men had made themselves useless by drinking whiskey. Furthermore, countless Indians suffered from diseases that the whites had introduced but could not cure. Even the earth around them looked scraped and stricken. The old harmony among people, animals, and land was lost. Some Cherokees feared that they were being punished for abandoning their ancient ways.

People began to have strange dreams and visions telling them to go back to the old ways. As The Ridge told McKenney, one group claimed they saw ghostly horsemen in the sky, who said to them,

> [The Great Spirit] is dissatisfied that you are receiving the white people in your land without distinction. You your-selves see that your hunting is gone—you are planting the corn of the white people—go and sell that back to them and plant Indian corn and pound it in the manner of your forefathers; do away with mills. The Mother of the Nation has forsaken you because all her bones are being broken through the grinding.

Many Cherokees took these ghostly messages to heart. They turned away from the Christian missionaries and began again to perform their ancient ceremonies and dances. They threw white people's corn into fires. Young Cherokee women burned their cotton dresses.

TECUMSEH.

The great Indian resistance leader Tecumseh inspired rebellion among the Creeks in 1812. According to a white opponent, Tecumseh was "one of those uncommon geniuses which spring up occasionally to produce revolutions and overturn the established order of things."

Just as this trend—later called a Ghost Dance movement—was reaching a peak, another rose to coincide with it. Tecumseh, a brilliant and charismatic chief of the Shawnee Indians to the north, was trying to rally all the Indians east of the Mississippi together against the whites. His message of Indian unification was strengthened by such movements as the Ghost Dance. Tecumseh traveled to each of the eastern tribes, trying to win their support. "Kill the cattle, the hogs and fowls; do not work, destroy the wheels and looms, throw away your ploughs and everything used by the Americans," he said at the Creek capital Tuckabatchee. "Sing the songs of the Indians of the Northern lakes and dance their dance. Shake your war clubs, shake yourselves, you will frighten the Americans." When Tecumseh threatened to stamp his foot and shake the earth because one Indian group refused to join him—and within a few weeks a devastating earthquake indeed struck along the Mississippi River— many were convinced.

But when Tecumseh appealed to the Cherokees, The Ridge refused to join him. He did not see the point in stirring up trouble. Furthermore, The Ridge himself was married to a white woman, and many of his followers were part white. They had reason to fear Tecumseh's movement.

At this point circumstances conspired to make action necessary: the United States again went to war with England. Some Indian bands—such as those Creeks known as Red Sticks because of their warriors' vermilion-painted war clubs—responded to Tecumseh with enthusiasm. These groups saw an opportunity to resist the white settlers, as had another group of Indians almost 40 years before in the revolutionary war. Other bands, such as the Cherokees led by The Ridge, thought it would be wiser to side this time with the United States. For the

Cherokees this would mean fighting their neighbors, the Red Stick faction of the Creeks. So in 1812 peace ended. The Cherokees joined the U.S. Army under a new officer, Andrew Jackson.

In October 1813, Sequoyah traveled the 20 miles between Willstown and Turkeytown and enlisted. He was to fight in one of the bloodiest and most decisive clashes in the war: the Battle of Horseshoe Bend.

In March 1814, Sequoyah and his company met about 1,000 Creeks entrenched along a sharp bend in the Tallapoosa River, 100 miles south of Willstown. Jackson's men fired repeatedly, but their attack had little effect on the dug-in warriors. Impatient, the Cherokees swam across the river and seized the Creeks' canoes, trapping them. The battle raged for five hours. Finally, the beleaguered Creeks leaped into the water, but the Cherokee and U.S. troops pursued them. Only 50 Creeks survived.

What followed was one of the grislier episodes of early American warfare. The Cherokees, like many other Indians, traditionally scalped their victims; scalps were war trophies. The white soldiers went beyond this, cutting off long strips of the dead Creeks' painted skin to weave into belts or reins.

And the soldiers' conduct did not improve. Discharged, they returned home before the Cherokee soldiers, marching north to Tennessee through Cherokee country. Along the way they smashed down Cherokee fences, stole horses and corn, shot livestock, and terrorized children, old people, and women. Sequoyah and the other Cherokee warriors who returned from war to find this destruction were deeply embittered. Jackson, no friend of the Indians, denied all of it and refused to make amends.

Americans continued to fight the British for another year, but Tecumseh had been killed and the Red Sticks defeated. The Cherokees returned to their civilian lives. For Sequoyah this meant, finally, marriage. In 1815 he married Sally Benge, a full-blooded Cherokee woman in her mid-twenties who was pretty, slim, and tall and who seemed to admire his skills as an artist and craftsman.

General Andrew Jackson quells insubordination in the ranks during the Creek campaign. Jackson's iron will brought his troops to victory despite frequent lapses in their morale.

He had distinguished himself in the war and so had acquired political status, too, perhaps ranking now as a chief. He built a cabin for his wife and himself. Now he would really begin his writing project.

Many accounts exist of this phase of Sequoyah's life, none of them known to be accurate. A favorite version, in which Sally plays a central role, is offered by Major George Lowrey, a Cherokee chief and a relative of Sequoyah's, who eventually dictated the story to a white historian. Before the war, Sequoyah had begun to make small picture-words (today called *pictographs*). Now, according to Lowrey, he resumed his work, creating quick symbols for the things around him: tree, house, pan, river, fire, child, cow, turkey. Every day he turned out dozens of little images on scraps of birchbark. Soon he had hundreds.

As the scraps of bark piled up, Sally grew concerned. Sequoyah was spending more time at this strange occupation and less time helping her in the fields or running his smith shop. He even built a small cabin away from their house, where he kept all his scraps and worked late at night under the light of pine torches. Sally began to suspect that he was demented—or, worse yet, practicing witchcraft.

Sequoyah, meanwhile, labored on. He discovered after a while that he could not use pictures for all the words in the Cherokee language. Pictures would only work with nouns, words that name objects, animals, places, or people. But no picture could represent "cook" or "run" or "die." And no picture could mean "quickly" or "thoughtful" or "almost." Sequoyah pondered this problem.

Then he tried a new tactic: he drew symbols that did not necessarily look like anything but that stood for something, like a pattern in a wampum belt. These new symbols, more abstract than pictographs, would today be called *ideographs*. For each word, Sequoyah invented a symbol: "quickly," for example, might have been a spiral, as the Algonkian Indians had drawn. When he had created this new system, he set to work again, once more turning out hundreds of little marks on his birchbark.

When he had drawn about a thousand of these, however, he discovered yet another problem. There were so many symbols that he could not always remember what he had meant when he drew them. It would have been like inventing a code but not having a way of recording what the code meant; after a time, it could not be cracked. Several years had gone by, and now this system, too, had proved a failure.

By this time Sally was not the only person who worried about Sequoyah. People in Willstown had also noticed that he was shirking his responsibilities and spending all his time alone in a cabin making incomprehensible marks on pieces of bark. John Ross, who later became the Cherokees' principal chief, rode by Sequoyah's cabin one day with a friend whose Cherokee name was Gallegina but who called himself Elias Boudinot. Boudinot later wrote of this experience. "There, in that cabin, resides George Guess, who has been . . . attempting to invent an alphabet," Ross told Boudinot. "He has been so intensely engaged in this foolish undertaking, that he has neglected to do other labor, and permitted his farm to be overrun with weeds and briars."

On another day, Lowrey recalls, Sequoyah's friend Turtle Fields told him that people thought he was wasting his life and making a fool of himself. To this Sequoyah replied:

> It is not our people that have advised me to this and it is not therefore our people who can be blamed if I am wrong. What I have done I have done from myself. . . . If I am no longer respected, what I am doing will not make our people the less respected, either by themselves or others; and so I shall go on and so you may tell our people.

But most people still agreed with Sally. If Sequoyah had become a lunatic, that was a shame. But if he had become a witch, that was dangerous. Sequoyah was not a shaman and should not meddle in their secret business. Something should be done.

So one night Sally acted. When Sequoyah stepped out of the cabin for a moment, she ran in and set fire to his work. Whether he was a lunatic or a sorcerer, this would put an end to it. When he returned to see his flaming cabin, however, he shrugged. That system had not worked; he had to start all over anyway.

By this time, in 1816, the war with Great Britain had ended. Andrew Jackson had scored a celebrated victory over the British in New Orleans and was hailed as a hero. He now turned his attention to settling with the hostile Creeks. He soon demonstrated that he was a harsh treaty maker, wresting two-thirds of their land from the Creeks—only half of whom had fought the United States, the other half serving under Jackson himself. Part of the land that he claimed from the Creeks in fact belonged to his allies the Cherokees.

The Cherokees protested this injustice, but by then Jackson, like other anti-Indian government officials, knew how to get what he wanted. He threatened even worse land cessions; he bribed; he convinced the Indians that he would ultimately get their land anyway. A minority of the Cherokee chiefs yielded, exchanging some of their eastern land for land that would be theirs "forever" in Arkansas. According to the treaty, anyone who wanted to go to Arkansas would be given certain supplies; those who remained east would become citizens—although citizens who could not vote.

At this point, even more changes had taken place in Cherokee country. In 1816 a missionary organization, the American Board of Commissioners for Foreign Missions, which supported Indian rights and a humane Indian policy, decided to send a battalion of missionaries into Cherokee country to accelerate their "progress." Unlike the earlier government agents, who had concentrated on getting the Indians to farm rather than hunt, the missionaries focused on the Cherokees' language and religion. They believed that Indians must become Christians and shed their native language. English, they said, was the key to civilization. After the Indians learned it, they would be able to read the Bible and other Christian works. One official named Pickering even said, "The Indian tongue is the great obstacle to the civilization of the Indians. The sooner it is removed the better."

To Sequoyah this must have sounded like a death knell. Once his people gave up their language, they gave up, essentially, their own thinking. He saw no reason for them to do this. The Cherokees were not inferior to the whites. When they had a written language, they, too, would be able to store and accumulate their knowledge, and they would become more powerful. But his work to create a Cherokee writing seemed doomed.

In light of his people's suspicions of him, his wife's anger, the government's endless pressure to acquire Cherokee land, settlers' constant harassment, and now the missionaries' determination to extinguish his people's language, Sequoyah was doubtless unhappy in his homeland. When Jackson asked him, with others, to accept land in Arkansas in place of land in the east, he agreed. Sequoyah marked the treaty under the name George Guess.

In 1818 about a thousand more Cherokees left the east. Sequoyah may have been among them, or he may have gone a year or two later after signing yet another treaty. He did not bring his family, perhaps planning to do so after he had settled. The emigrants left on flotillas of

keelboats, shallow vessels usually used for freight. They traveled down the Tennessee, Ohio, and Mississippi rivers and up the Arkansas River, finally settling on the north side of the Arkansas in what is now Pope County, Arkansas. The journey took about 70 days.

In the new territory, the settlers could live as they chose. Some wore European clothing; others, like Sequoyah, stuck to Cherokee clothes. Most kept small farms or orchards, and many again took up hunting and continued to perform the traditional tribal dances and rituals. Here at last Sequoyah could be comfortable and resume his work.

But he had still not designed a system that would work. There were too many objects in the world for him to picture, and for many words he could not use pictures at all. If he tried to make a symbol or code for each word, sooner or later there would simply be too many to remember.

Settlers navigate the Arkansas River. Sequoyah and about 1,000 other Cherokees traveled by water into their new territory west of the Mississippi.

Sequoyah racked his brain. He sat for days on end in his new cabin, smoking his pipe, staring vacantly at the fields and woods and hills around him. He gazed blankly, listening as if dreaming to birds singing, dogs yelping, children playing, people talking. He could not solve the riddle.

Then, suddenly, he did it.

Sounds. Language was made up of sounds. He spoke a few words to himself. Each was made up of a sequence of different noises. For instance, the name for his people comprised three different sounds: tsa-la-gi. He did not need a picture of a Cherokee to mean that; nor did he need some arbitrary symbol. He needed some way of capturing the sounds: tsa-la-gi. For more than a decade he had been chasing the wrong idea. He did not need to *look* at the world to create a written language. He needed to *listen*.

Excitedly, Sequoyah gathered up his materials. Sitting in his cabin, he muttered out loud all the words he could think of. Each word he broke into sounds, or syllables, seeing how his mouth shaped different noises, the *tsa* sound hissing behind his teeth, the *ga* sound deep in his throat. For each sound he made a symbol. Soon he discovered that many of the sounds were repeated in other words. This was wonderful: he would not need as many symbols as he thought. He visited people, listening intently to them. Sometimes he would nod suddenly when he heard a sound that he had not yet caught, pull out his bark and charcoal, and make a new mark. Everyone thought Sequoyah was crazier than ever.

But in a month he had invented a way to write Cherokee.

SE - QUO - YAH

6

Sequoyah's Talking Leaves

Sequoyah, inventor of the Cherokee syllabary, displays his work. Arriving in Washington in 1828, Sequoyah was greeted with interest and admiration by those who had learned of his accomplishment. This portrait commemorates his visit.

The system Sequoyah invented is called a syllabary. This is like an alphabet, but instead of using letters as the smallest units, it uses whole syllables. This means, for example, that the word for Cherokee requires only three characters, one for each syllable, instead of eight letters. Sequoyah's syllabary has 86 different characters. Sequoyah drew the symbols for his syllabary from different letters he had seen—Roman letters used in English writing and Greek letters—and from his imagination. But the letters he borrowed had nothing to do with the sounds they represented in those other languages. The character that looks like a Roman "D," for example, in Cherokee stands for our *ah* sound.

Once he had designed this system, his next task was to make his syllabary presentable. No one who saw his rude scratching on bark would believe him any more than they ever had. So Sequoyah acquired from a trader some paper and a pen, making ink from bark the way that he had made paint before as an artist. He reproduced his syllabary in careful printing on the paper and then set out to convince his people.

71

Luckily, the Cherokees in the west were more tolerant of Sequoyah than those in the east had been. At first, as he expected, they ignored him and did not want to look at his strange—possibly black magic—marks. But he managed to persuade a friend to listen. The syllabary was easy, and Sequoyah's friend learned it so quickly that he could no longer doubt. Soon Sequoyah was able to teach others his syllabary, and before long many of the western Cherokees knew it, marveling at Sequoyah's brilliant invention.

But this was the easy part. The challenge would be persuading the majority of the tribe, still in the east, to accept his invention. If he could quickly convince them that they did not need the whites' language and writing, perhaps he could halt the English and Christian forces that were transforming his people. He knew the easterners mistrusted him because—on top of seeming demented or evil—he had agreed to unpopular treaties. He would have to act quickly and carefully. He decided to travel east and to bring with him letters from the westerners—printed in Sequoyan—as testimony.

When he arrived in eastern Cherokee country in 1822 he read the letters aloud. His listeners scoffed; they thought he had simply stored certain speeches in his mind as he had always stored ancient stories. But after spending time with his family, Sequoyah realized that his six-year-old daughter Ahyokeh was an excellent student—and a valuable ally. In almost no time she had not only learned the syllabary but had suggested improvements. Sequoyah knew that she could help him convince the tribe.

He arranged to meet with some of the principal chiefs. Arriving with Ahyokeh, he described his project in detail. Again, they turned away. But then Sequoyah asked them to try an experiment: he sent Ahyokeh away and asked the chiefs to make some specific remarks, which he carefully wrote down. Then he called Ahyokeh back and

This chart contains the letters of the Cherokee alphabet, as invented by Sequoyah. In the mid-19th century, as the syllabary came into extensive use, printers changed some of the original characters to fit existing type, and the alphabet began to look more Roman.

Cherokee Alphabet.

D a	R e	T i	Ꮹ o	O u	i v
S ga Ꭷ ka	F ge	Y gi	A go	J gu	E gv
Ꮹ ha	Ꭾ he	Ꭿ hi	F ho	Γ hu	Ꮽ hv
W la	Ꮯ le	P li	G lo	M lu	Ꭷ lv
Ꮳ ma	Ꮈ me	H mi	Ꮷ mo	Y mu	
Ꮟ na Ꮕ hna Ꮐ nah	Λ ne	h ni	Z no	Ꮹ nu	O nv
Ꮖ qua	Ꮺ que	Ꮙ qui	V quo	Ꮰ quu	Ꮛ quv
Ꮜ sa Ꭲ s	4 se	b si	Ꮧ so	Ꮈ su	R sv
Ꮤ da W ta	S de Ꮦ te	Ꮧ di Ꮨ ti	Λ do	S du	Ꮸ dv
Ꮪ dla Ꮣ tla	L tle	C tli	Ꮬ tlo	Ꮅ tlu	P tlv
Ꮆ tsa	V tse	Ᏼ tsi	K tso	Ꮷ tsu	C tsv
Ꮐ wa	Ꮺ we	Ꮩ wi	Ꮿ wo	Ꮽ wu	6 wv
Ꮝ ya	Ᏸ ye	Ꭹ yi	Ꮵ yo	G yu	B yv

Sounds represented by Vowels

a, as *a* in *father*, or short as a in *rival*
e, as *a* in *hate*, or short as *e* in *met*
i, as *i* in *pique*, or short as i in *pit*

o, as *aw* in *law*, or short as o in *not*.
u, as *oo* in *fool*, or short as u in *pull*.
v, as *u* in *but*, nasalized.

Consonant   Sounds

g nearly as in English, but approaching to k. d nearly as in English but approaching to t. h.k.l.m.n.q. s.t.w.y. as in English. Syllables beginning with g. except Ꮝ have sometimes the power of k. Ꭷ.Ꮝ.Ꮙ. are sometimes sounded to, tu, tv. and Syllables written with tl except Ꮣ sometimes vary to dl.

gave her what he had written. Quickly and easily, the child read out the chiefs' very words. They were astonished—but even then not certain that this was not some witch's trick.

After lengthy deliberation, however, the chiefs agreed to another test. They summoned some of the brightest young men and asked Sequoyah to instruct them. He and his new pupils immediately set to work. Soon the students were proficient, and at the appointed time, Sequoyah, his students, and the chiefs again met. This time the chiefs invented the tests, which were very rigorous. The young men were moved far from each other and given complex messages to write down. Then these notes were carried by messenger—and all of them were easily read. The chiefs could not help but be convinced. Sequoyah had succeeded.

Sequoyah thus invented a way of writing—something no other individual in the history of the world is known to have done. In only a decade he reproduced the process from spoken to written language—a job that whole cultures, such as the Sumerians and Greeks, had taken centuries to accomplish. To the Cherokees, Sequoyah's achievement seemed like a miracle, but he had other views. When someone said to him that he had been taught by the Great Spirit, Sequoyah replied, "I taught myself." He meant that there was nothing magical about writing. Like wheels or guns, it was an invention.

Because the system was so quick and easy to learn and because so many Cherokees—discouraged by the constant pressure to change—rejoiced at finding a system in their own language, it was immediately popular. Once someone knew it, he or she could easily teach another. If they had no paper or pens, they could use what they did have. Soon messages were appearing everywhere, drawn on walls, trees, roads, the sides of buildings. In 1824, one missionary said, "The knowledge of Mr. Guess's Alphabet is spreading through the nation like fire among the leaves." Soon more than half the adults in the Cherokee Nation were literate in Sequoyan—a higher level of literacy than in any other nation at the time, including the United States.

The General Council of the Cherokee Nation voted to present Sequoyah with a silver medal. It was inscribed

"Presented to George Gist by the General Council of the Cherokee Nation, for his ingenuity in The Invention of the Cherokee Alphabet, 1825." Beneath the inscription were two crossed pipes and a portrait of Sequoyah.

By then Sequoyah had returned to Arkansas. This time he brought letters written by Cherokees in the east to their friends and families in the west. He had created a way to join people separated by miles, to capture his people's language and thoughts, and, he hoped, to preserve his people's identity by giving them a way to record their ideas, laws, history, knowledge, and legends.

Sequoyah had given his people—not those who had adopted white ways and understood English better than Cherokee, but those who wished to go back to the old life—a source of pride and unity. Many shamans, whose job it was to preserve the tribe's traditions, immediately began to record their prescriptions and chants in Sequoyan.

But just as Sequoyah's invention was hailed by many, it was also seen as a threat. Missionaries were disturbed to see that the system had given their rivals, the shamans, a valuable tool for promoting "pagan" Cherokee culture, with its wild dancing and strange beliefs about the natural world. They were determined to continue teaching English and ridding their students of their Cherokee heritage.

But after a few years they saw that this was impossible: Sequoyan was so much easier to learn. Students could learn it in only a few days while sitting outside on a riverbank with a friend. Besides, as the missionary Samuel Worcester observed, the patriotic Cherokees were proud of Sequoyah's invention. By the end of the 1820s, the missionaries decided that they would no longer resist Sequoyah's syllabary. If they could not bring the

Cherokees to the English Bible, they would bring the English Bible to the Cherokees. They began to translate it and print it in Sequoyan.

Meanwhile, many of the important chiefs at this time were half white and could barely understand Cherokee. These chiefs saw English as the wave of the future and were not interested in the "backward" Cherokee language. They were busy making Cherokee culture more like white culture.

By the late 1820s John Ridge, the half-blood son of The Ridge; John Ross, another part-Cherokee; and other important chiefs were making a great many changes to further assimilate the eastern Cherokees. After Tahlonteskee had threatened the tribe with removal 10 years earlier, these younger chiefs had decided to convince the U.S. government that they were sufficiently "civilized" to live alongside their white neighbors. They had begun to create a white-style government with a bicameral council (resembling the U.S. Senate and House of Representatives) and a system of courts with juried trials.

In 1824 they had laid out a new capital, New Echota, to replace Echota, which had been all but destroyed in the warfare of the late 1700s. This new capital, located in present-day Georgia, looked nothing like a traditional Cherokee town. Its council house had two floors, a staircase, glass windows, plank floors, and brick chimneys. Around it ran smooth streets with large frame houses, shops, and taverns. The men who founded it, along with others who had prospered, owned plantations, elegant brick homes, and slaves. They educated themselves and their children at northeastern boarding schools and imported many of their household goods from the North as well.

What remained was for the Cherokee Nation to take one final step toward assimilation: to draft and adopt a constitution like that of the United States. A constitu-

John Ridge, who helped to frame the Cherokee Constitution, posed for this portrait in 1826. Ridge embraced white culture, but he also campaigned actively on behalf of his people, making many trips to Washington, D.C., to defend Cherokee land claims.

tional convention was organized, and representatives were chosen. However, most of the representatives were wealthy, English-speaking half-Cherokees, and the constitution they proposed was to be written in English and to contain laws that many of the other Cherokees felt had nothing to do with them—laws about property rights, when they had no property, and about new marriage ceremonies. Worst of all, it was to embrace Christianity.

Many Cherokees resented the constitution. They did not feel they needed it, and they did not like these new encumbrances that would help only the wealthy chiefs. So again, as in 1810, a Ghost Dance movement arose among those who longed for the old days when tribal decisions were made after lengthy communal discussion and when the people could count on each other to help in difficult times. People rebelled; they held late-night dances around fires; they had visions and dreams. A story

John Ross strikes a European pose. Like Sequoyah, Ross fought under Jackson in the Battle of Horseshoe Bend. In 1828, he became principal chief of the Cherokees.

circulated about a woman who had given birth to triplets, all of them with a full mouth of teeth; the eldest infant was said to have immediately criticized the mother in Cherokee for abandoning the old ways.

These critics of the new capital thought that now that they had their own form of writing, they could write their own truly Cherokee constitution—one that would not have half as many complicated, unnecessary laws. In a development that the missionaries and U.S. government officials might have feared, Sequoyah's syllabary became a sort of underground, secret code. The rebels wrote letters to each other across distances in Sequoyan. They held a special council, largely under the leadership of a chief named White Path. They began to draft in Sequoyan their criticisms of the proposed English constitution.

But they could do nothing. Sequoyah's syllabary had arrived too late to be a part of the Cherokee government. English was already the official language, and assimilation had progressed too far. After a brief series of protests, these new traditionalists gave up. The official Cherokee Constitution was completed in English in July 1827. Its preamble read:

> We, the Representatives of the Cherokee Nation, in Convention assembled, in order to establish justice, ensure tranquility, promote our common welfare, and secure to ourselves and our posterity the blessings of liberty: acknowledging with humility and gratitude the goodness of the sovereign Ruler of the Universe, in offering us an opportunity so favorable to the design, and imploring His aid and direction in its accomplishment, do ordain and establish this Constitution for the Government of the Cherokee Nation.

Despite this particular failure of the syllabary, Sequoyah took satisfaction in another achievement it made possible. Elias Boudinot—a nephew of The Ridge, one-sixteenth white, elegant, with a dark complexion and

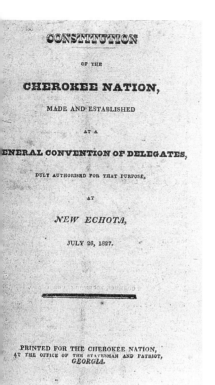

CONSTITUTION

OF THE

CHEROKEE NATION,

MADE AND ESTABLISHED

AT A

ENERAL CONVENTION OF DELEGATES,

DULY AUTHORISED FOR THAT PURPOSE,

AT

NEW ECHOTA,

JULY 26, 1827.

PRINTED FOR THE CHEROKEE NATION,
AT THE OFFICE OF THE STATESMAN AND PATRIOT,
GEORGIA.

The Cherokee constitution, written in 1827, was modeled on the constitution of the United States. Many Native American tribes eventually adopted constitutions of this kind.

dark hair, who had been extensively educated in the Northeast—arranged to have a press created so that he could print a newspaper for the Cherokees. It was to be half in English, half in Sequoyan, and it would provide a forum for Cherokee news and ideas. Called the *Cherokee Phoenix*, the newspaper was first printed in February 1828. It was the first Indian newspaper ever printed and soon attracted readers from all over the country, and even in Europe.

Sequoyah was now considered a successful—even brilliant—man. Indeed, he had become a spokesman for his people. By now white settlers had pushed so far west they had not only reached the Cherokees in Arkansas but had gone around them. As they had done in the east, the settlers were regularly ignoring Indian borders and claiming Cherokee land. In December 1827 the Cherokees elected Sequoyah one of a group of delegates to travel to Washington to discuss this problem.

Sequoyah and his companions arrived in the capital in the spring of 1828. The *Cherokee Phoenix* had just come out, and Sequoyah was an immediate celebrity. He had his portrait painted by the artist Charles Bird King and was interviewed by countless journalists, among them Samuel Knapp, who was at the time a well-known author. A typical section of his work read:

> No stoick could have been more grave in his demeanor than was See-quah-yah; he pondered, according to the Indian custom, for a considerable time after each question was put, before he made his reply, and often took a whiff of his calumet while reflecting on an answer. . . . I have seldom met a man of more shrewdness than See-quah-yah. He adhered to all the customs of his country; and when his associate chiefs on the mission, assumed our costume, he was dressed in all respects like an Indian. See-quah-yah is a man of diversified talents; he passes from metaphysical and philosophical investigation to mechanical occupations with the greatest ease.

But there was more to do in Washington than be admired. Sequoyah and his fellow delegates had come in hope of getting a treaty to halt the intrusions of settlers on their land. But as so often happened, they wound up doing something altogether different. Before they left the capital, they had signed a new treaty, ceding Cherokee land in Arkansas for "permanent" Cherokee territory in Oklahoma. Sequoyah and the three other delegates signed the treaty with the characters of his syllabary.

When he departed Washington in 1828, Sequoyah left behind a Cherokee Nation vastly different from the one in which he had grown up. After half a century of struggle, the assimilationists had triumphed. They had transformed their people's ways—their clothes, beliefs, and language—to match those of the whites around them. They had created a new capital modeled on the white cities they had seen. They had written a Cherokee constitution very much like that of their white neighbors.

The front page of the Cherokee Phoenix included columns in both Cherokee and English. The paper printed the laws of the nation, news, Bible passages, editorials, and advertisements.

Washingtonians enter and leave Brown's Indian Queen Hotel, the usual stopping place for Cherokees visiting the capital to negotiate on behalf of their people. Sequoyah made his first trip to Washington in the spring of 1828.

The Cherokees had every reason to believe that their nation had become "civilized" and would finally enjoy a secure, stable position in the United States.

Yet the Cherokees' problems were not over: in 1829, Andrew Jackson became the seventh president of the United States.

7

A Snake in the Grass

In 1829, Sequoyah moved with his family and several thousand other Cherokees to the southern part of the new Indian Territory, in what is now Oklahoma. Similar to their homeland, this new country may have appealed to Sequoyah and his compatriots. Oklahoma, said the visiting Prussian Count de Pourtalés, had "the most beautiful stretches of forest that I have ever seen . . . magnificent, sparsely scattered trees . . . some bright green and others delicately shaped and turned red by the frost."

Sequoyah and his family settled in the hilly, forested Ozarks section of the new territory, between the Sallisaw Creek and Lees Creek. Here they built a simple rectangular log cabin with a pitched roof and a stone fireplace. Like the other Cherokees settling up and down the creek, Sequoyah and his family started a small farm, where they grew corn, potatoes, peas, beans, melons, and pumpkins and where they kept small herds of cows, horses, and hogs.

During the 10 years after his invention, Sequoyah lived quietly with his wife and children. (Apart from Ahyokeh and a son, Tessee, the names and birthdates of Sequoyah's children are not known. It is said that he and Sally had several.) By this time he was in his mid-fifties. He was

President Andrew Jackson strikes a commanding pose in this James B. Longacre engraving, derived from an 1820 painting by Thomas Sully. Jackson's Indian Removal Bill destroyed all hope for the Cherokees' peaceful existence in their Georgia homeland.

still interested in spreading the knowledge of his alphabet and willingly instructed anyone who came by to learn. He traveled occasionally to different settlements in the west and taught groups of Cherokees his system of writing. He also continued his old pleasures: sitting for hours with friends and acquaintances, telling stories, explaining to children the ideas and legends of the ancient Cherokee people. And he wrote constantly in his journal.

In the meantime, Sequoyah was able to follow the lives of the "civilized" eastern Cherokees by reading the *Cherokee Phoenix*. The paper's first issue had announced its policy:

> The laws and public documents of the Nation, and matters relating to the welfare and condition of the Cherokees as a people, will be faithfully published in English and Cherokee. . . . We will invariably state the will of the majority of our people on the subject of the present controversy with Georgia, and the present removal policy of the United States Government.

Eastern Oklahoma is depicted as a place of abundant wildlife and delicate, pastoral beauty in Thomas Nuttall's illustration from his Journal of Travel into the Arkansas Territory. *In 1829, Sequoyah and his family set up a farm in this region.*

Elegant buildings dominate this 1837 view of Savannah, Georgia. Although the Cherokees attended well-known schools, used an American system of government, and had their own smooth streets lined with European-style shops and houses, few Georgians considered them their cultural equals.

For with Andrew Jackson's election to the presidency, the eastern Cherokees again found themselves fighting for their land. Jackson, unlike his six predecessors, from Washington to John Quincy Adams, had always despised Indians. Along with the frontiersmen among whom he had grown up, he claimed that it was impossible for Indians to be "civilized."

By 1828 the Cherokee Nation, with its elegant plantations, educated leaders, newspaper, and brand-new capital, was in many ways even more "civilized" than its neighbor Georgia. This, however, only threatened and infuriated the Georgians. As they saw it, they had fought the British for the land occupied by the Cherokees, and they were entitled to it. In this sentiment they had valuable support, both from Jackson and from the Georgia Compact, an 1802 federal document that promised the extinction one day of all Cherokee land claims in Georgia. The Georgians had not yet made much use of this document, but at the end of the 1820s—when gold was discovered on Cherokee land—they decided the time had come.

The state quickly passed a series of laws aimed at pushing the Cherokees out of the Southeast. The new legislation began:

> It is hereby ordained, that all the laws of Georgia are extended over the Cherokee country. . . . That all laws, usages and customs made and established and enforced in said territory, by said Cherokee Indians, be . . . declared null and void.

In addition, the laws provided for the confiscation of the Cherokees' land, the removal of their rights, and the prohibition of their meeting in council or digging for gold on their own property. When any Cherokees continued these activities—or, worse, resisted the Georgia Guard who tried to prevent them—they were thrown into jail.

Bad as it was, the situation got worse. In May 1830, President Jackson persuaded Congress to pass his Indian Removal Bill, which called for the exile of the 60,000 Indians of the five eastern tribes to territory west of the Mississippi. The bill shocked and outraged not only the affected Indians but people throughout the country, including congressmen, lawyers, missionaries, newspaper editors, and other public figures. One representative, Vermont's Horace Everett, spoke passionately before Congress:

> This policy cannot come to good. It must and will depress, dishearten, and crush [the Indians]. . . . It is all unmingled, unmitigated evil. There is evil on the other side, but none commensurate with that of this compulsory removal.

Despite the public outcry, President Jackson proceeded. In December 1830 he justified his position to Congress, saying:

It will separate the Indians from immediate contact with settlements of whites; free them from the power of the States; enable them to pursue happiness in their own way, and under their own rude institutions; . . . and perhaps cause them gradually, under the protection of the Government, and through the influence of good counsels, to cast off their savage habits, and become an interesting, civilized, and Christian community.

By 1832, Jackson had persuaded four of the Five Civilized Tribes—Chickasaw, Choctaw, Creek, and Seminole—to sign treaties providing for their own removal. But the Cherokees, long considered the most "civilized" of the five, refused to yield.

In this the Cherokees were led now by their new principal chief, John Ross. He was in his late thirties, a short and slight man, blue-eyed, brown-haired, the son and grandson of white men. He dressed in white men's clothing—although he sometimes wore a turban—but was extremely popular among his people, both rich and poor. Outraged by the Removal Bill, many white lawyers and public figures—among them, constitutional lawyer and former attorney general William Wirt—came to Ross's aid. These supporters believed that because the Cherokees were a separate, sovereign nation, they were immune from the laws of Georgia as well as from any removal laws. The United States needed to deal with the Cherokees as with any other sovereign nation, through treaties. It would be up to the Supreme Court to support this contention.

In an 1831 case called *Cherokee Nation v. Georgia*, Wirt asked the Supreme Court to recognize the sovereignty of the Cherokee Nation and to deny Georgia's authority. But Chief Justice John Marshall, although sympathetic, wrote for the court that "an Indian tribe or nation within the United States is not a foreign state in the sense of the Constitution, and cannot maintain an action in the Courts of the United States."

Missionary and Indian advocate Samuel Austin Worcester helped make Sequoyah's syllabary suitable for printing. An active supporter of Elias Boudinot's Cherokee newspaper, Worcester also translated the Bible and hymns into Cherokee.

This was a great blow. Fortunately, the Cherokee Nation had allies. In March 1831, Sequoyah would have read this item in the *Cherokee Phoenix*:

> The law of Georgia, making it a high misdemeanor for a white man to reside in the Cherokee Nation, without taking an oath of allegiance, and obtaining a permit from the Governor of Georgia, or his agents, is now in course of execution. On last Sabbath, after the usual time of divine service, the Georgia Guard arrived and arrested . . . Rev. Samuel A. Worcester.

Worcester, long a friend of the Cherokees, had refused to take the oath of allegiance to the state of Georgia. This new development—the arrest of a white man on behalf of the Cherokees—provided an opportunity for publicity and another Supreme Court case, *Worcester v. Georgia*. Perhaps the Indians in the Cherokee Nation had no rights, but it was inconceivable that a white man had none, either. If the Cherokees could prove that Georgia's laws had no just power over Worcester, a resident of the Cherokee Nation, they could prove that Georgia's laws likewise had no power over the Cherokees.

The Cherokees won their case. In 1832, John Marshall, with the other justices, decided that the state laws of Georgia had no authority over the Indians. "It is glorious news," wrote Elias Boudinot. "The laws of the state are declared by the highest judicial tribunal in the country to be null & void. . . . The question is forever settled as to who is right & who is wrong."

But other Cherokee leaders were less optimistic. As John Ridge put it, "Chicken Snake Genl. Jackson has time to crawl and hide in the luxuriant Grass of his nefarious hypocrisy." Indeed, as if to prove him right, Jackson reportedly said, "John Marshall has rendered his decision; now let him enforce it."

Just as the colonial settlers had ignored their British government in the 1760s and the American frontiersmen had ignored their fledgling U.S. government in the 1780s, so now the Georgians, encouraged by President Jackson, ignored the Supreme Court decision. The state waited almost a year before releasing Samuel Worcester and then proceeded with its distribution of Cherokee land, dividing it into lots and selling it to Georgians.

Up until this point the eastern Cherokees had been united in their aims. But when the Supreme Court seemed to have no power over the actions of citizens and even of the president, many Cherokee leaders became discouraged. Among these were Elias Boudinot; The Ridge, or Major Ridge, as he was now called; and John Ridge.

They finally began to believe—as had Old Tassel, Doublehead, and Tahlonteskee before them—that the tribe would be more likely to survive if it yielded.

Boudinot and his cousin John Ridge, after all, had reached the apex of what the whites called civilization. They dressed as impeccably as any white gentlemen. They had studied in northeastern boarding schools. They were Christians. They had helped create a nation's constitution and newspaper. They were married to white women. Yet, simply because they had Indian blood, they were refused the rights of citizenship or political autonomy. So, hesitantly, Boudinot began to publish in the *Phoenix* editorials in favor of removal.

The move brought an end to Boudinot's career. Cherokee politics did not allow for dissent, and those who differed from the majority were expected to withdraw. The Chickamaugans half a century before had been obliged to leave the tribe because they intended to continue fighting when the others did not. In August 1832, Boudinot resigned the editorship of the *Phoenix*. In his final issue he wrote,

> I love my country and I love my people . . . and for that very reason I should deem it my duty to tell them the whole truth, or what I believe to be the truth. I cannot tell them that we will be reinstated in our rights, when I have no such hope.

A less experienced man took over, and the *Phoenix* eventually sputtered to a halt in 1834.

By 1834 many of the Cherokees had been dispossessed, their lands auctioned off by lottery. Even Chief Ross, returning from a mission to Washington, discovered that he no longer owned his fine plantation. Yet he continued to rally the Cherokees and to attempt to negotiate with the U.S. government. But Boudinot and the Ridges thought it was impossible to remain any longer. Like so many others before them, they decided—for the good,

Elias Boudinot, editor of the Cherokee Phoenix, *was educated in white boarding schools and retained many of the values of European culture.*

they thought, of the Cherokee Nation—to negotiate for a generous treaty. In March 1835 they met secretly with U.S. officials at Boudinot's elegant home in New Echota and signed a treaty yielding all remaining Cherokee lands for territory in the west and $5 million.

Major Ridge, who had helped assassinate Doublehead, knew well what he was doing: "I have signed my death warrant," he declared. And Boudinot, who later wrote about the crisis, knew as well: "We can die but the great Cherokee Nation will be saved."

Despite Ross's desperate efforts to have this treaty nullified, in the spring of 1836 the U.S. Senate ratified it by a single vote. President Jackson signed it immediately, and the U.S. government gave the Cherokees until May 1838 to remove.

The "Treaty Party," those who had signed the Treaty of New Echota, emigrated at once. Ross, however, continued to make his case in Washington. He and his supporters—the remaining 16,000 Cherokees—still believed that they could prove the invalidity of the Treaty of New Echota.

Finally, Ross saw that he was helpless. The Cherokee Nation had been sold. The best he could do was befriend Major General Winfield Scott, the officer charged with overseeing the Cherokees' removal. In this he succeeded: Scott commanded his troops to show the Indians "every possible kindness."

A few Cherokees escaped, fled into the mountains, and formed what is still called the Eastern Band of Cherokees. For the others, however, the terrible removal process began in June 1838 and continued into the fall. Although many of Scott's men did follow his humane orders, others did not; the roundup was accompanied by robbery, brutality, rape, and even murder. John Burnett, a private in Scott's army, described the final days:

> I saw the helpless Cherokees arrested and dragged from their homes, and driven by bayonet into the stockades. And in the chill of a drizzling rain on an October morning I saw them loaded like cattle or sheep into six hundred and forty-five wagons and started toward the west. . . . Chief Ross led in prayer and when the bugle sounded and the wagons started rolling many of the children . . . waved their little hands good-bye to their mountain homes.

The nation set off in 13 different detachments, some on keelboats—as Sequoyah had traveled 20 years earlier—some on carts or horseback, some on foot. They journeyed through rain, sleet, and snow along muddy, treacherous paths, carrying whatever remnants of their homes they could. They had scanty clothes, few blankets, and almost no shoes. The army provided them with dirty campsites and poor food, and many soon fell sick. They

Cherokees make their painful journey westward in Robert Lindneux's rendering of the Trail of Tears. The Cherokee exodus, during which at least 4,000 people died, has become a symbol of the long, tragic history of relations between Native Americans and the U.S. government.

suffered from diarrhea, dysentery, head and chest colds, measles, and pneumonia.

In late March the Cherokees finally arrived in the new western territory. No more than 12,000 of the original 16,000 people had survived the journey; some historians suspect that barely half the tribe made it. The rest had died of sickness, exposure, or violence and been hastily buried along the way—in the tragic journey that was thereafter called the Trail of Tears.

8

Sequoyah's Last Letters

In the late 1830s the Cherokee Nation West covered about 7 million acres of land, with present-day Missouri to the northeast and Arkansas to the west. The western Cherokees—the Old Settlers—lived mostly on fenced farms. In the capital, Tahlonteskee (named after Sequoyah's uncle, who had first come west 30 years before), the Indians had a council house in which they elected their three chiefs, council members, judges, and police. This government was far looser than that of the Cherokee Nation East. It contained few written laws and no constitution. The life of the western Cherokees was much more rustic and traditional than the easterners' life had been.

When the eastern emigrants reached the west in the spring of 1839 they were dirty, demoralized, exhausted, sick, and poor. All had lost loved ones on the journey. Most had no cooking or farming utensils, and the food they were supplied in their new settlements was often inedible: meat that had gone bad or flour infested with weevils. For these people—many of whom had owned comfortable homes and farms back east—life in the new territory was like a dark, bewildering dream.

The newcomers began settling in all around the Old Settlers, pitching tents, clearing ground, constructing

A statue of Sequoyah, commissioned by the state of Oklahoma in 1917, stands in the U.S. Capitol.

95

huts. Assimilation would not be easy, for friction among the various groups had long existed. The new emigrants led by Ross resented the Old Settlers, who had, they thought, abandoned the Cherokee Nation. And they detested the members of the Treaty Party, the Ridges and Boudinot, who, they believed, had betrayed them. Major Ridge presented a particular problem: not only had he led in the assassination or expulsion of an earlier generation of treaty signers—many of them now Old Settlers—but he had signed the infamous Treaty of New Echota. In addition to all this, there remained the fundamental differences between the Cherokees who had adapted to white culture and those who had not. Sequoyah, as so often before, stood between these factions.

In June 1839, the Old Settler chiefs, Sequoyah among them, invited Ross to a meeting in Takattokah, about 40 miles northeast of Tahlonteskee and Sallisaw, so that they could formally welcome the easterners. The chiefs assumed that Ross would naturally accept the government that they had long ago established in the west. But Ross had a different idea: because he and his people formed a majority, he said, a new government should be created. This government would replicate that of the eastern

Sequoyah, making another new start in 1830, built this cabin in Indian Territory. He and his family had been living in Oklahoma for 10 years when the eastern Cherokees arrived.

Cherokees and would entail a written set of laws and a constitution. Ross, of course, would play an important part in it.

The western chiefs were startled to hear this proposal. They had no need for a new government; theirs was fine, and there was no reason for Ross not to accept it, as had all previous emigrants. Sequoyah, however, who felt that Ross had made an important point, tried to persuade the western chiefs to consider Ross's proposal. The Treaty Party members counseled them to reject it. The western chiefs angrily refused the proposal and adjourned the meeting. But just before the groups dispersed, Sequoyah and an easterner named Bushyhead intervened and got both factions to agree to meet again in a few weeks, when tempers had cooled.

The Treaty Party members' role in the debate, however, on top of the tragedy that they—according to the emigrants—had caused, was enough to heat simmering resentments to the boiling point. The day after the council adjourned, before dawn, three men wearing masks pulled John Ridge from his bed. They dragged him out to the yard, where more masked men waited. There, as his horrified wife and children watched, he was stabbed 25 times, and his throat was cut. A messenger then rushed to overtake John's father, Major Ridge, on his way to Washington, to warn him of danger. He found the old man lying on the road with five bullets in his head and body. And later in the morning, as Elias Boudinot worked on his new house, a group of men came to him asking for assistance. As he turned to fetch what they wanted, they stabbed him in the back and then slashed his body and hacked at his skull with tomahawks.

Frightened by this turn of events, the territory's white U.S. agents tried to cancel the new council scheduled for July 1, but Sequoyah and Ross ignored them. On the

appointed day, about 2,000 Cherokees met at the Illinois Camp Ground. Although many eastern delegates attended, the western delegates were still angry, and few of them came. Sequoyah himself served as the temporary president of the western Cherokees. His first act was to write, in his own syllabary, letters to the western chiefs:

> We, the old settlers, are here in council with the late emigrants, and we want you to come up without delay, that we may talk matters over like friends and brothers. These people are here in great multitudes, and they are perfectly friendly towards us. They have said, over and over again that they will be glad to see you and we have full confidence that they will receive you in all friendship. There is no drinking here to disturb the peace . . . and we have no doubt but we can have all things amicably and satisfactorily settled.

Sequoyah's letters succeeded in bringing one of the western chiefs, but not the others, who stayed away and held their own convention. Nevertheless, those who attended the Illinois convention on July 12 drafted a landmark Act of Union:

> We, the people composing the Eastern and Western
> Cherokee Nation, in National Convention assembled, by
> virtue of our original and inalienable rights, do hereby sol-
> emnly and mutually agree to form ourselves into one body
> politic, under the style and title of the Cherokee Nation.

This Act of Union was probably read aloud by Sequoyah, in Cherokee, to the assembled people. It was then signed by him, as president of the western Cherokees, and by George Lowrey, as president of the eastern Cherokees.

The Act of Union was to provide the basis for the eventual Cherokee government. It did not do so, however, for several more years. In the meantime, factionalism kept the new Cherokee Nation in a state of near civil war.

Sequoyah by now was nearly 70 years old. Twenty years earlier he had given his people an extraordinary gift—the ability to write so that they could preserve their identity and build their strength as a people. Now he had done his best to mend the sharp rifts between them; if they were not yet ready to seal those rifts themselves, they would be ready eventually. Sequoyah returned to his family, his farm, and his teaching.

Around this time—in the early 1840s—Sequoyah had many visitors, for he had become almost a legend since his invention. Some of these visitors published their impressions of the old man. John Howard Payne, who was writing a history of the Cherokees, met Sequoyah at Chief Ross's new house in Indian Territory. He later described the celebrated Cherokee:

> Guess had a turban of roses and posies upon a white
> ground girding his venerable grey hairs;—a long dark blue
> robe, bordered around the lower edge and the cuffs, with
> black;—a blue and white minutely checked calico tunic
> under it, confined with an Indian beaded belt, which sus-
> tained a large wooden handled knife, in a rough leathern
> sheath;—the tunic open on the breast and its collar apart,

with a twisted handkerchief flung around his neck &
gathered within the bosom of the tunic. He wore plain
buckskin leggings; and one of a deeper chocolate hue than
the other. One of his legs [is] lame and shrunken. His moc-
casins were ornamented buckskin. He had a long dusky
white bag of sumac with him, and a long Indian pipe, and
smoked incessantly, replenishing his pipe from his bag. His
air was altogether what we picture to ourselves of an old
Greek philosopher. He talked and gesticulated very grace-
fully;—his voice alternately swelling,—and then sinking to
a whisper,—and his eyes firing up and then its wild flashes
subsiding into a gentle & most benignant smile.

Even as he approached old age, however, Sequoyah
remained restless. His whole life had been spent making
things—a milk house for his mother; drawings and
paintings admired by his people; buckles, bridles, and
ornaments; his masterpiece, the syllabary; and then
treaties and agreements. All his work had been aimed at
improving his people's lives, uniting them, and
strengthening the Cherokee identity. At 70 he was not
ready to stop. He knew that there was still work for him
to do. One day in the summer of 1842, Sequoyah, with
his son Tessee, a friend named The Worm, and a few
others, set out on a mission. The Worm later told the
story to a Cherokee journalist.

"My friend," Sequoyah said to The Worm at the start
of their journey, "I desire to reach the Mexican country."
Of the Cherokees who had gone to Texas, one group had
moved on to settle in Mexico. Most likely Sequoyah
intended to urge them to join him in developing the new
Cherokee Nation.

The trip from what is now Oklahoma to Mexico was
difficult, and Sequoyah was old and ill. He and his group
moved slowly on horseback across country they were not
sure of, traveling south across the Arkansas River and
then the Red River, moving from there to the village of
Echasi. Early in the trip a band of Tewockenee Indians

stole their horses, forcing them to continue on foot. But they also met with kind, hospitable Indians, many of whom had heard of Sequoyah and his invention. Each time they stopped, Sequoyah wrote more in his journal.

More than once, the group left Sequoyah behind to rest while they traveled ahead to find out if they were near the Mexican Cherokees. Not only was Sequoyah's leg troubling him, but he was weak, had a pain in his chest, and often could eat only honey, plums, and bread. When they reached San Antonio, some months after starting their journey, the group once more left the old man safely in a cave with a good supply of honey and venison.

The others went ahead, finally reaching a Cherokee village lying in a grove in a Mexican prairie, a few miles from a place called San Cranto. These Cherokees were delighted to meet them and immediately offered to go to Sequoyah and convey him to their village. When the group made it back to the cave where they had left the old man, however, they found that he had disappeared. The Worm later said:

> Arriving at the cave, we . . . discovered a log of wood lean-ing against a tree, and a letter bound to one of its limbs. The Letter was written by Sequoyah in his own native lan-guage, and informed us that, after being left alone, he had met with misfortune—the water having rose very high, drove him from his retreat and swept away his store of provisions and almost everything else; that, under these cir-cumstances he had determined to pursue his journey; that if not too long absent we would be able to find him.

Only 20 years earlier, had Sequoyah tried to leave a "letter," it would have been as silent and meaningless as the cave's stone walls.

They followed his tracks—easily identified because of his limp—and a few days later found him "in the centre of a thicket in the forks of the river . . . seated by a lonely fire." To survive until that point he had shaved the remaining meat from some deerskins, constructed a raft to cross the Mauluke River, and chopped down a tree to obtain honey from a comb in its branches. For each day his companions had been gone he had cut a notch in an oak tree. Sequoyah had lost none of the skills he had learned as a boy. Unfortunately, however, he had lost the journal in which he had been recording thoughts and events ever since his invention. Rejoined with his friends and son, Sequoyah traveled on toward the Cherokees in Mexico.

Although Sequoyah may indeed have reached the Mexican Cherokees, he never returned to the Cherokee Nation. In April 1845 the Cherokee National Council, which was planning to go in search of the old man, learned that he had "departed this life in the town of Sanfernando in the month of August 1843."

Sequoyah's life spanned one of the most complex and difficult periods his people would ever experience. Faced with a powerful, seemingly inexorable opponent, the Cherokees were compelled either to yield or to resist. Yet even this choice was more complicated than it looked: both yielding and resisting could take many forms. The Cherokees could try to maintain their traditional life and homeland by fighting a constant and probably losing battle. They could instead abandon their homeland and retain their traditional life elsewhere. Or they could conform to the ways of their opponents, abandoning not their land but their traditions.

In Sequoyah's own family were powerful chiefs—Old Tassel, Doublehead, Tahlonteskee—who advocated each of these tactics in turn, and Sequoyah matured to see each approach tried. But one by one the strategies failed. Slowly he realized that what the Cherokees faced was more than an enemy; it was their very extinction. What was at stake was not merely his people's land or power. It was their culture, language, beliefs, and knowledge — their very flesh, blood, and spirit. Sequoyah came to see that a totally different tactic was needed to save his people's culture.

Sequoyah's great contribution to the Cherokees was the invention of a tool to hold that culture fast. He believed that with a written language the Cherokees could preserve their tribal identity, collect and advance their knowledge, record their histories, and, he hoped, bind themselves together in a way that would allow them to resist the changes eroding them as a tribe.

Unfortunately, Sequoyah's invention could not stop the radical transformation of his people. Although in one decade he had accomplished what it had taken entire cultures centuries to produce, his invention came too late to help his people preserve their homeland and traditional life.

Yet his syllabary did arrive in time to do much. It gave people separated by half a continent a way to communicate. It inspired the creation of a tribal newspaper—something never before achieved. Almost overnight, it converted an unlettered people into the most literate nation of its time. And it gave a people on the very edge of crisis a vital jolt of hope.

Sequoyah was recognized for his accomplishment within his own lifetime. But recognition of his singular contribution increased after his death. In 1851 the neighborhood where he had made a living before his trip to Mexico was renamed Sequoyah District, and the larger area was subsequently called Sequoyah County. Later, the giant California redwood was named for him, and in 1902 the Sequoyah League was established to improve conditions for all Native Americans. In 1917 the state of Oklahoma presented the United States with a statue of

Sequoyah, which still stands in the Capitol, and in 1927 a monument to the inventor was erected near the old *Cherokee Phoenix* office in New Echota. A few years later, the Oklahoma Historical Society restored Sequoyah's home in the old Indian Territory.

In October 1843, just a few months after Sequoyah died, the Cherokee National Council authorized the creation of a new national newspaper, the *Cherokee Advocate*, modeled on the original *Cherokee Phoenix*. This paper, dedicated to advancing the Cherokee cause and edited by John Ross's nephew, was first published in September 1844. Like the *Phoenix*, half its columns were printed in English, the other half in Sequoyan. The newspaper continued publication until 1906—one hundred years after Sequoyah first envisioned his people writing in their own tongue.

But what may be Sequoyah's greatest legacy is a work that has its roots in the middle of the 19th century, when a young Cherokee named A'yuníni embarked on a special

Editors and printers produced the Cherokee Phoenix *in this shop at New Echota, Georgia.*

Swimmer, photographed in 1887, used Sequoyah's syllabary to transcribe hundreds of traditional Cherokee songs, stories, chants and remedies.

project. Born just before the Cherokee removal, A'yuníni, or Swimmer, had been part of the Eastern Band whose members had escaped with their families to the North Carolina hills. There he had been brought up as a shaman. Like Sequoyah, Swimmer loved his people's ancient traditions, stories, rituals, and songs, and he honored their unique knowledge of their land and the plants and animals that filled it. And like Sequoyah, he wished to preserve these things.

A'yuníni learned Sequoyah's syllabary. One day he began to collect and write down all the chants, prescriptions, songs, histories, and legends he could find. Soon he had written hundreds of "talking leaves." And today, long, long after Sequoyah's death in Mexico, long after Swimmer's burial in the hills near old Echota, the "talking leaves" continue to tell the story of the Cherokees, the people to whom Sequoyah dedicated his rich and productive life.

CHRONOLOGY

ca. 1773   Born in Tuskegee in present-day Tennessee

1777   Sequoyah's uncle Doublehead and his followers secede to Chickamauga

1792   Sequoyah's family moves with Chickamaugans to Willstown in present-day Alabama

1801   Sequoyah travels to Echota and begins to develop the idea of inventing a writing system

1810   Sequoyah's uncle Tahlonteskee moves west to start a new Cherokee nation; Sequoyah begins work on writing project

1813   Enlists to fight under General Andrew Jackson against Red Stick Creeks

1815   Marries Sally Benge, a young Cherokee woman

1816   Signs treaty ceding eastern Cherokee territory for land in west

1818   Emigrates to Arkansas Territory

1821   Completes Cherokee syllabary, the first native North American writing system

1825   Awarded medal by Cherokee General Council in honor of invention

1827   Cherokee Constitution adopted

1828   Sequoyah travels to Washington to defend Cherokee land claims in Arkansas Territory; first edition of the *Cherokee Phoenix* appears, with articles written in English and Cherokee

1829   Sequoyah moves to new Indian Territory in eastern Oklahoma

1830   President Andrew Jackson passes Indian Removal Bill

1838   Cherokees begin forced migration known to history as the Trail of Tears

1842   Sequoyah sets out for Mexico

1843   Dies in San Fernando, Mexico

FURTHER READING

Claro, Nicole. *The Cherokee Indians*. New York: Chelsea House, 1992.

Cwiklik, Robert. *Sequoyah and the Cherokee Alphabet*. Morristown, NJ: Silver Burdett, 1989.

Hunt, Bernice Kohn. *Talking Leaves: The Story of Sequoyah*. New York: Hawthorne Books, 1969.

Kilpatrick, Jack Frederick, ed. and trans. *The Shadow of Sequoyah*. University of Oklahoma Press, 1965.

Lepthien, Emilie U. *The Cherokee*. Chicago: Childrens Press, 1985.

McCall, Barbara A. *The Cherokee*. Vero Beach, FL: Rourke Publications, 1989.

Mariott, Alice Lee. *Sequoyah: The Leader of the Cherokees*. New York: Random House, 1956.

Patterson, Lillie. *Sequoyah: The Cherokee Who Captured Words. Champaign*, IL: Garrard Publishing Company, 1975.

Perdue, Theda. *The Cherokee*. New York: Chelsea House, 1989.

Petersen, David. *Sequoyah, Father of the Cherokee Alphabet*. Chicago: Childrens Press, 1991.

Radford, Ruby Lorraine. *Sequoyah*. New York: Putnam, 1969.

INDEX

PICTURE CREDITS

JANE SHUMATE studied classical literature and mythology at Princeton University and creative writing at Columbia University. She has also written *Sojourner Truth and the Voice of Freedom*, another book for young readers. Shumate lives in New York, where she teaches and is working on a novel.

W. DAVID BAIRD is the Howard A. White Professor of History at Pepperdine University in Malibu, California. He holds a Ph.D. from the University of Oklahoma and was formerly on the faculty of history at the University of Arkansas, Fayetteville, and Oklahoma State University. He has served as president of both the Western History Association, a professional organization, and Phi Alpha Theta, the international honor society for students of history. Dr. Baird is also the author of *The Quapaw Indians: A History of the Downstream People* and *Peter Pitchlynn: Chief of the Choctaws* and the editor of *A Creek Warrior of the Confederacy: The Autobiography of Chief G. W. Grayson*.